2018 Key Stats

For the S&P, DJIA and NASDAQ

Daily Detail of the Major Indices

With Limited but Pertinent Anecdotes

Stephen Kirby

ISBN: 978-0-578-45939-4

To my exceptional and adorable wife Nancy, and our children and grandchildren

Acknowledgements

I am especially appreciative of my wife, Nancy, who has been my guide and guardian for over thirty years. She has been a light in darkness and always encouraging during our life together.

I am also grateful to the highly skilled and knowledgeable staff and contributors at StockCharts.com. They don't know me from Adam but have guided me with the charts, analysis and commentary that membership provides. I highly recommend a visit to this website. Many of the site's offerings are free and will quickly get you hooked on the fundamentals of charting and technical analysis.

The first time I ever heard of technical analysis was in college during the early 70s. Professor Fitzpatrick taught a course on investment analysis that included point and figure charting, my first exposure to T/A. There was no VisiCalc, Lotus 1-2-3 or Excel in those days so we charted stocks on graph paper by hand.

Introduction

Excerpt
8/30/18

"If you want to be something really scary for Halloween dress up like a tariff! The markets were basically digesting recent gains when someone on CNBC said "tariff" at around 3:00 pm. It was as effective as yelling fire in a crowded theater because the indices all took a header and ended lower on the day."

2018 had the good, the bad and the ugly for anyone with a portfolio. If you were 50 or younger and did nothing to conserve your invested principal you will likely not remember what happened this year and in particular the last calendar quarter, five years from now. If you are older than 50 you will remember the setbacks incurred in your portfolio unless you only invest in cash or near-cash instruments. It was an especially painful last quarter for those invested in equities and bonds for that matter; because most positions suffered unless you were skillful in managing your portfolio or had an active manager doing so for you.

This book details daily open, high, low and close often with variances from the prior day's market close for most but not all trading days. I also provide a reasonable narrative that provides some insight when possible, that explains the day's outside activities that may have affected the trading results. I haven't found any publications that might already provide this information in a similar manner. It is intended as a reference that can be used in years to come and geared to those that enjoy historical, factual detail.

I refer almost daily to "my T/A and P&F sums" and the VIX. The basis for the sums originates in the StockCharts.com Predefined Scans section found on the home page and includes the sections of Bullish and Bearish Technical Indicators and Bullish and Bearish Patterns. I have been summing equity totals from each separate section and include the totals in a spreadsheet that I have been keeping since March, 2016.

Date COB	Bullish Tech Indicators	Bullish P&F Patterns	Chart Results Daily Favorable	Bear Tech Indicators	Bear P&F Patterns	Unfavorable	Fav vs Unfav Ratio
3/28/16	1532	1739	3271	1808	1281	3089	1.0589
3/29/16	1674	1738	3412	1666	950	2616	1.3043
3/30/16	5345	1752	7097	1498	1301	2799	2.5355
4/1/16	3108	1955	5063	1303	1104	2407	2.1034
4/4/16	2349	1978	4327	1615	1091	2706	1.599

When the rightmost column is 1 or greater it means that the majority of firms included in the scans are in a technically bullish position. it is risk-on as long as the VIX is 15 or less.

When the right most column is between .75 and one and the VIX is starting to rise it is a caution indication. When the ratio is less than .75 it indicates corrective sentiments and if below .50 possibly bigger issues are at play and I become defensive. This is especially when the VIX is moving higher while the ratio is moving lower.

I know that you'll find this book a good historical read and reference. It explains my view and any concerns with each market close and avoids being tedious to read. All of the numbers have been rounded.

Table of Contents

January

1/02/18

S&P and Nas closed at all-time new highs. Dow just shy of hitting most recent high. Russell is shy of all time high. Staying the course at least through Thursday because there is nothing negative about today's results. NG had closed about its 50-day moving avg. on Friday and was above its 200-day moving avg. $WTIC closed above (just by a squeak) its 50 day moving avg. Last time it was above it was around Sept 2014.

The S&P opened at 2684 (+10) and reached a closing high of 2696, up 22.

The Dow opened at 24809 (+90) and reached a high of 24864 (+145) before closing at 24824, up 105.

The Nas opened at 6938 (+35) and reached a closing high of 7007, up 104.

1/03/18

Going through the charts tells me to do nothing today. The S&P ended higher after another all-time high. The DOW hit a new high but closed below it. My one technical concern is that the P&F chart for the S&P met it's several month price objective of 2699. So now what happens? Staying the course seems appropriate because there is no logic yet for any correction. A good sign too is that the VIX closed at 9.15 which is well below the 50 and 200 Day SMA. WTIC closed at 61.63 for a +2% gain.

The S&P opened at 2698 (+2) and hit a high of 2714 (+18) before closing slightly off the high at 2713, up 17.

The Nas opened at 7017 (+10) and hit a high of 7069 (+62) before closing at 7066, up 59.

1/04/18

Three major indices hit new all-time highs before settling back. Biggest news was the DOW 25,000 breakthrough.

Going to stay the course for most if not all of tomorrow. The 9th falls on Tuesday and is a down day about 20% of the time. Mondays often of late have been down days too so I may take some funds from S&P and put them in the PLUS fund. Not sure at this time. As for the bull mkt it is still hitting on all cylinders. Even though most everything is in the oversold (70+) RSI area the buyers keep coming in.

The S&P opened at 2719 (+6) and hit a high of 2729 (+16) before closing at 2724, up 11.

The Dow opened at 24965 (+42) and hit a high of 25106 (+183) and closed above 25000 for the first time at 25075, up 152.

The Nas opened at 7090 (+24) and reached 7098 (+32) before closing at 7078, up 12.

1/05/18

The indices continued firing on all cylinders throughout the day with new all-time highs being reached. It may be getting top heavy now and some at StockCharts.com are getting very uneasy, especially with the rate of climb (basically parabolic) that has been occurring. Correction coming?

The S&P opened at 2731 (+7) and also reached a new high at 2743 where it closed, up 19.

The Dow opened at 25115 (+40) and hit its new high of 25300 (+225) before closing at 25296, up 221.

The Nas opened at 7106 (+28) and reached a new high of 7137, up 59. It closed at the high of the day.

1/8/18

The S&P and Nasdaq closed at new highs. Dow down but barely. Going through my charts I am finding that not much has changed. since Thursday narrative. On Friday I moved funds from the mid/small index fund to the Harbor International fund because the results were better and international funds seem to be back in the bull market run.

The S&P opened at Friday's close of 2743 and reached a new high of 2749 (+6) and a low of 2738 (-5) before closing at 2748, up 5.

The Dow opened at 25308 (+12) and hit a new high of 25312 (16) and a low of 25235 (-61) before closing at 25283, down 13.

The Nas opened at 7135 (-2) and hit a high of 7161 (+24) and a low of 7124 (-13) before closing at 7157, up 20.

1/9/18

There are two highlights regarding the S&P and targeted technical highs. The first was met last week when the 2699 objective was met on a monthly point and figure chart that I watched for many years. The second objective was in a Murphy contribution in which he discussed the price target based upon the fifth wave of the Elliot Wave Theory. John Murphy pointed out that you determine the target price of the 5th wave by tripling the first wave up leg and add back the bear market bottom. The bottom was reached in the spring of 2009 at 666 and the first up leg topped at 1370. The difference is 704. Triple that is 2112 to which you add the 666 leaving you with a target price of 2778. Today it reached 2759 so I need to consider the importance of these two targets. Apparently, targets are often overshot but one needs to consider that we have not had any corrections to speak of for almost two years. Depending upon where the S&P heads tomorrow I may take some of the funds from S&P and put it in the PLUS fund because I don't have the option of opting out immediately but need to wait until the end of the day. We'll see. Beyond that the majors all hit new highs again today. Also, of interest was that WTIC had a high of 63.48 and closed at 62.96. My review of a P&F chart that I have had for years tells me that WTIC is now off to the races.

The S&P opened at 2751 (+3) and hit a new high of 2759 (+11) before closing at 2751, up 3.

The Dow opened at 25312 (+29) and hit its new high of 25440 (+157) before closing at 25386, up 103.

The Nas opened at 7174 (+17) and hit a new high of 7181 (+24) but also a low of 7148 (-9) before closing at 7164, up 7.

1/10/18

The morning started off in interesting fashion as the major indexes were all down right out the gate. The Dow was down 128 pts early on and the S&P around -15. Nas was down all day as well. The reasoning for this was that rumor had it that China was not going to be buying any more American debt instruments. But it was more likely simply profit taking. The markets closed lower on all fronts but just marginally so.

The S&P opened at 2746 (-5) and reached an intraday low of 2736 (-15) before closing at 2748, down 3.

The Dow opened at 25348 (-38) and reached a high of 25405 (+19) and a low of 25257 (-129) before closing at 25369, down 17.

1/11/18

The Dow finished up 206, S&P 20 and the NAS 58. Each finished at the high for the day. Beyond my technical concerns of the S&P cruising past the P&F target of 2699 and the fact that the S&P is only 11 points away from the Elliott Wave target of 2778. My sense tells me to take funds out of S&P and put it to the PLUS. This way I'm not as extended and still can make decent daily amounts. Any technician will tell you that the market is overheated and needs to pause and yet some of the best moves up and coming during this month. We'll see. I will watch the markets carefully in the morning before deciding what to do next.

The S&P opened at 2753 (+5) and hit a new high of 2768 where it closed up 20.

The Dow opened at 25399 (+30) and hit a new high of 25575 and closed there, up 206.

The Nas opened at 7169 (+15) and hit its new high of 7212 where it closed, up 58.

1/12/18

Stop me if you have heard this before; the Dow was up 228 to finish the week at 25,803. The S&P was up 18.67 to finish at 2786.23 and the NAS was up 49.28 to finish at 7261.06…record closes again. I may have been hasty in decreasing the S&P fund balance, but it did make me a little more comfortable. I will look for at least a 3% correction and other guidance before putting money back into the fund.

The S&P opened at 2770 (+2) and reached a new high of 2788 (+20) before closing at another record close of 2786, up 18.

The Dow opened at 25638 (+63) and hit a new high of 25810 (+235) before closing at 25803, up 228 for a new closing high.

The Nas opened at 7208 (-4) and reached a new high of 7265 (+53) before closing at a record high of 7261, up 49.

1/16/18

Today started off gang-busters but ended up being short lived. The Dow climbed to 26086 before reversing to close at 25793 and the Nas climbed to 7330 before closing at 7223. The S&P climbed to 2807 intraday and closed at 2776.Volume was very high in each of the indexes.

The S&P opened at 2799 (+13) and hit a new high of 2808 (+22) and a low of 2769 (-17) before closing at 2776, down 10.

The Dow opened at 25988 (+185) and reached a new high of 26086 (+283) and a low of 25703 (-100) before closing at 25793, down 10.

The Nas opened at 7307 (+46) and hit a new high of 7330 (+69) and a low of 7206 (-55) before closing at 7224, down 37.

1/17/18

Today closed up on the S&P but reached an intraday high of 2807 before closing at 2803. This piqued my interest because it represented a double top although it was not stretched out at all. Still, I take it for a sign of fatigue. The Dow closed at 26116 for the first close over 26000 and the Nas was back over 7300 but closed at 7298.

The S&P opened at 2785 (+9) and reached a high of 2807 (+31) before closing at 2803, up 27.

The Dow opened at 25911 (118) and reached a new high of 26130 (+337) before closing at 26115, up 323.

The Nas opened at 7258 (+34) and reached a high of 7309 (+85) before closing at 7298, up 74.

1/18/18

Today was a basically quiet one. The Nas had a new intraday high of 7314 but closed at 7296. The Dow lost 98 points but still closed above 26000. The S&P closed at 2798, down 4.5 points. Volumes for these indices was slightly above average. Tomorrow should be an interesting day because of the threat of a government shutdown. My guess is that the dems will blink first and we'll end up with the Senate passing another CR for a month. It will be interesting if the opposite happens and if so, I would expect a correction of sorts. Would like to see at least 5% before putting more cash to work.

The S&P opened at 2802 (-1) and hit 2806 (+3) and a low of 2793 (-10) before closing at 2798, down 5.

The Dow opened at 26150 (+34) and hit a high of 26153 (+37) and a low of 25947 (-169) before closing at 26018, down 98.

The Nas opened at 7294 (-4) and reached a high of 7314 (+16) and a low of 7276 (-22) before closing at 7296, down 2.

1/19/18

Friday is usually an interesting day because all issues are weighed by investors who have to go two days without trading and they want to be sure that their investments are safe. Because this particular Friday involved a closing without knowing if there would be a CR or shutdown, my expectations was that the market indices would all close down. Instead each closed at the day's high.

The S&P closed at the high of the day at 2810, an increase of 12 points from yesterday and a new all-time high. It opened at 2803 (+5).

The Dow closed at 26072 up 54 from the prior day after spending the day basically in the red. It opened at 25987 (-31) and hit a low of 25943 (-75) before closing at its high.

The Nas closed at 7336 also the high of the day as well as a new all-time high. It opened at 7312 (+16)

before closing up 40.

Today was significant because the unknown outcome of a Senate vote at the close demonstrated just how strong this market bull is and that more funds are flowing into equities. This unknown would have been troubling to the market in the past. Just surprised and glad I still have half of our funds in equities.

1/22/18

It was another record setting day for the major indices with the Dow closing at 26215, up 143; the S&P closing at 2833, up 22.68 and the Nas closed at 7408 which was up 72.

These are clearly interesting times with high RSIs (Relative Strength Index) the new norm for the time being.

The S&P opened at 2809 (-1) and reached a low of 2808 (-2) and a new closing high of 2833.

The Dow opened at 26025 (-46) and a low of 25975 (-97) before reaching its new closing high 26215.

The Nas opened at 7338 (+2) and hit a low of 7333 (-3) before reaching its closing high.

1/23/18

Today proved interesting in that the markets started out with significant gains and then tanked at around noon when Mnuchin publicly stated at DAVOS that the U.S. was pleased with a weak dollar. There is really nothing new about the slowly sinking dollar but the fact that it was broadcasted at DAVOS make it seem like breaking news.

The S&P opened at 2635 (+2) and hit a new high of 2842 (+9) and a low of 2831 (-2) before closing at 2839, up 6.

The Dow opened at yesterday's close 26215 and reached a new high of 26246 (+32) and a low of 26144 (-71) before closing at 26211, down 4.

The Nas opened at 7425 (+17) and reached a new high of 7465 (+57) before closing at 7460, up 52.

1/24/18

All of the indices reached record highs again. The S&P got as high as 2853 and ended up at 2838. The Dow was as high as 26392 before closing at 26252. The Nas was at 7486 at its peak and closed at 7415.

WTIC was higher on the day closing at 65.61. Still looking for it to cross the $70 mark in the very near future. Some of the reason for the increase can be attributed to the falling dollar.

The S&P opened at 2845 (+6) and hit 2853 (+14) and a low of 2825 (-14) before closing down 1 at 2838.

The Dow opened at 26282 (+71) and achieved its high of 26393 (+182) and an intraday low of 26107 (-104) before closing up 41 points.

The Nas opened at 7474 (+14) and reached its record high of 7486 (+26) and a low of 7377 (-83) before closing at 7415, down 45.

1/25/18

Both the Dow and S&P closed at record highs although the S&P closed just .12 higher than Tuesday's close of 2839.13. The Dow closed at 26392. Much of the day saw the major indices trying to find firm ground after opening higher. Nothing new to speak of regarding the markets and direction. There appears to be no reason not to be fully invested.

The S&P opened at 2846 (+8) and hit a high of 2849 (+11) and a daily low of 2831 (-7) prior to closing at 2839, up 1.

The Dow opened at 26313 (+61) and hit a record high of 26458 (+206) before closing at 26393, up 141.

The Nas opened at 7458 (+43) and hit a high of 7459 (+44) and a low of 7389 (-26) before closing at 7411, down 4.

1/26/18

Friday was quite a day for the major indices. All closed at record highs and at the high for the day. The S&P closed at 2873 for a gain of 34; the Dow closed at 26617 for a gain of 224 and the Nas closed at 7506 for a gain of 95 points.

The S&P opened at 2847 (+8) and hit its new high at the close. The Dow opened at 26467 (+74) and closed at its high for the 224 point gain. The Nas opened at 7448 (+37) and closed at its high as well. This kind of Friday action is unusual and obviously traders have no fear going through the weekend.

1/29/18

Today saw mostly corrections. The Dow lost 177; the S&P 19 and the Nas 39. With the exception of the Dow, volumes were slightly higher than on Friday. Significant? Maybe but it is hard to say if it was due to selling or buying, something I'll have to research. I'm frankly glad to see some buying relief after this great start to the year. For now, everything stays as it is with no portfolio changes planned.

The S&P opened at 2867 (-6) and hit a low of 2851 (-22) before closing at 2854, down 19.

The Dow opened at 26584 (-33) and reached an intraday low of 26435 (-182) prior to its close of 26439, down 178.

The Nas opened at 7484 (-22) and hit a low of 7456 (-50) before closing at 7467, down 39.

February

2/06/18

Since my last entry the markets demonstrated "shock and awe" that was not dissimilar to that I watched

when the Iraq War began in March 2003. The contributors at StockCharts.com had been warning members that the parabolic rise of the major indices was unsustainable and it played out as such over a five-day period beginning January 30, when the S&P closed down 32 points, the Dow 362 points and the Nasdaq 65 points.

January 31 saw small gains and February 1, a mixed day of no significance. Then on Friday, February 2, all hell started to break loose with the Dow down 666 (prophecy), the S&P down 60 and the Nasdaq finishing down 145!

What a way to start the weekend!

Feeling helpless throughout was not fun nor was worrying about it. I figured we were experiencing a 3% (at worst) pullback, much the same as we have been seeing since the November election. To top it off, the folks at StockCharts.com were declaring that the markets should expect an across the board drop that included anywhere from 3% to 10% or possibly worse. At any rate, I had been enjoying a 4% increase in our 401 balance in less than a one month period and dreaming of increasing it by half before the year ended. Like all other investors watching the futures on Sunday night and expecting something positive, I realized the sh*t still hadn't hit the fan!

February 5, Monday, was as frantic a day as I have ever witnessed since investing. The S&P opened at down at 2741 and hit an intraday low of 2638, closing at 2649, 113 points from Friday's close. The Dow opened at 25338 and hit an intraday low of 23924, down from the Friday close by 1597 points. The index then gained back some of the ground but closed at 24346, down 1175 from the Friday close. The Nas didn't fare much better closing at 6968, down 273. Over a five day period the major indices basically lost 10%, something that normally takes weeks or months to occur.

Tuesday saw some return to normalcy with gains across the board as you might expect, given what had just happened. The S&P closed at 2695, up 46, the Dow closed up at 24912, gaining 566 points and the Nas closed up 148 points closing at 7116. The S&P hit an intraday low of 2593, the Dow hit 23778 intraday and the Nas hit 6825 for an intraday low. The fun isn't over but hopefully the bottoms hit on Monday will become support across the boards.

2/07/18

The bulls and bears were having a tug-of-war today. The S&P opened at 2691, was as low as 2681 and finished at 2682, down 13 on the day. The Dow opened at 24893, was as low as 24785 and closed at 24893, down only 25. The Nas opened at 7086, was as low as 7052 and finished at 7052, down 64 for the day. All in all, discouraging. A state of flux seems to be status quo now. I was expecting to see a reasonable recovery of the indices and it isn't happening. I am sticking with the overall game plan now of waiting and seeing. This is an anxiety producing period, but the dramatic movement was not at all uncalled for.

2/08/18

Thursday, Feb. 8 was another tumultuous day. The swing for the S&P ran from a high of 2685 where it opened to an intraday low of 2581, (104 points) and closed at the low. The Dow's swing was between 24904 and 23849 the intraday low, (1055 points) and closed at 23860. The Nas had a high of 7074 and an intraday low of 6777 (297points), and like the S&P it closed at that low.

Simply another unbelievable day at the bourses within an unbearable drubbing since Thursday, Feb. 1st!

2/09/18

When it's pouring record amounts of rainfall you are told the system is causing the rain to "train" in the same location, day after day. That's our indices patterns now. Friday started the same as the previous five with either a big up or down open. The S&P opened higher only to lose ground throughout most of the day reaching a new intraday low of 2533. The Dow likewise opened higher at 23993 only to fade in the same manner as the S&P, hitting a new intraday low of 23360. The Nas opened at 6863 and proceeded down the same path as the other majors hitting a new intraday low of 6631.

Things started changing at about 1:45 across the board as volume picked up in the other direction and the indices started climbing. At day's end all three indices were higher. The S&P finished at 2619, up 39; the Dow finished at 24191, up 330 points; and the Nas finished at 6864 up 97. None of the majors finished at its high for the day, the only negative.

2/12/18

After a semi-tense weekend, the futures on Sunday night looked promising and that carried into the open today. The major indices all opened higher and remained positive throughout the day. The S&P opened at 2636 and closed at 2656, up 36, but off the high of 2672. The Dow opened at 24338 achieving an intraday high of 24765, up 410. The Nas opened up at 6937 moving as high as 7024 before closing at 6982, closing up 107. In two trading days the S&P has gained back 75, the Dow 740 and the Nas 204. That is a 3% increase from the Friday intraday low of 2533 for the S&P; a 3.2% increase from the Friday intraday low of 23360 for the Dow and a 3.1% increase from the intraday low of 6630 on Friday.

I ran the numbers (above) for three possible retracement and have more or less committed to going to almost all cash should the S&P hit the 50% value which is 2702. I have set an alert for 2685 and 24940 for the Dow. That retracement roughly corresponds to the 50-day EMA as well for the S&P.

2/13/18

Today I committed to going to the PLUS fund once the alerts that I had set were hit. For the S&P I used 2685 and for the Dow 24940. These are slightly below the calculated values shown in the chart above so that I could react in part before everyone else does and because ICMA won't make the transfers until after the markets close, which is fine. It isn't like you can immediately get in or out by placing an order with a broker.

The S&P opened at 2646 and hit an intraday high of 2669 before closing at 2663. That open was below the previous day's close of 2656. The Dow opened at 24540, down from the prior day close of 24601 and closed at 24640. The Nas opened at 6942 and closed at 7014.

The indices all opened down after the CPI came out with higher than expected results but corrected in the morning.

2/14/18

The indices opened lower but took off like scalded cats for the rest of the day. The S&P opened at 2651 and hit an intraday high of 2702 (within a fraction of the 50% retracement) before closing at 2699. That

was up 36 on the day. The Dow opened at 24536 and reached an intraday high of 24925 before closing at 24893, up 253 points. The Nas opened at 6979, reached 7152 before closing at 7144, up 130.

With the markets doing so well it was a little bit hard to stick to my guns and go to the PLUS fund. But after careful evaluation of the recent correction and best guess of a retest I followed my plan.

2/15/18

I began a spreadsheet in March of 2016 that is comprised of two sets of numbers that I record daily. The information comes from the StockCharts.com website home page under predefined scans that shows the counts of technical indicators. From this chart I sum four columns of numbers from bullish technical indicators, bearish technical indicators, bullish P&F patterns and bearish P&F patterns. I maintain a graph of a five-day moving average and a twenty-day moving average. The data for the graph is the sum of the bullish technical indicators and the bullish P&F patterns which is under the favorable column and I sum the bearish technical and bearish P&F patterns which is under the unfavorable column. A daily ratio is arrived at by comparing the daily results of the two columns. Since I began the spreadsheet the bullish P&F patterns sum has always well exceeded the bearish patterns sum with few exceptions. Beginning with Feb. 2, the bearish P&F sum has exceeded the bullish pattern by a good variance. These results are in line with the sentiment of some of the StockCharts.com contributors that we are in a bear market for at least the short term.

The indices all closed higher on the day. The S&P opened at 2713 and closed at the high for the day at 2731, up 32. The Dow followed suit opening at 25048 and closing at 25200, up 307. The Nas opened at 7201 and closed at 7256, up 112 points. I missed a gain in my 401 of around $1000 by transferring most of the funds to the

PLUS fund but am comfortable with having made the move based upon the 50% retracement.

2/16/18

By COB today you could tell the markets were exhausted after the bullish runup of the past six days. The S$P opened at 2727 and had an intraday high of 2754 before closing at 2732 for a gain of 1. The Dow opened at 25165 reaching an intraday high of 25432 (+267) before closing at 25219, up 19. The Nas opened at 7237 reaching an intraday high of 7303 (+66) before closing at 7239, down 17 points. This day is significant because the S$P and Dow intraday highs exceeded the 62% retracement values (see chart page 7) and couldn't hold the highs, both indices closing below the 62% value. The Nas closed above its value yesterday and today. I expect, based on today's action, that the market is going to retest its previous lows beginning Monday.

Technical analysis is very reliable when used properly and becoming a member of StockCharts.com is very confidence building because of the blogs of its skilled staff.

2/20/18

Yesterday's indices were pretty much lackluster throughout the course of the day and in line with technical expectations. I'm guessing a retest of the February 9 intraday lows before the indices get back into bull market activities.

The S&P opened at 2723 and reached an intraday high of 2738. The Fibonacci 61.8 value is around 2742, so the index needs to close above that in order to continue the bullish streak. The index closed at 2716. The story is the same with the Dow. Opening at 25125, it achieved a high of 25179 before closing at 24965, down 254. 25379 is the 61.8 retracement value for this index. The Nas opened at 7209 and reached an intraday high of 7296 before closing at 7234, down 5 points. Its 61.8 value is 7173 and is the only major index to close above it.

There are still no definitive courses of action that I can take now. I am keeping an eye on two bond related funds but waiting for some assurance that these are going to regain positive movement. The first is Western Asset Corp and the other is Pimco. I also review Nuveen Real Estate because it is technically showing signs of turning positive.

2/21/18

The S&P opened at 2721 and reached an intraday high of 2747 before closing at 2701, down 15 points from Tuesday's close. Not to be outdone, the Dow opened at 24988 and reached an intraday high of 25268 before closing at 24798, down from the prior close by 167 points. The Nas didn't want to buck the trend opening at 7258, reaching a high of 7339 before closing at 7218, down 16 points on the day. The S$P cannot close above 7243, the 62% retracement value nor can the Dow. Its retracement is 25379. The only major to do so and sustain it is the Nas.

The recent theme has been to open higher, rise higher intraday and close below the prior day close, the exception being the Nas.

The VIX was below 20 but needs to be at 16 or below before one can take comfort in a lower volatility market.

2/22/18

This week has seen the indices open higher, rise throughout the day only to move lower throughout the afternoon. Today was different in that the closes were slightly to moderately higher. The S&P opened at 2710 reaching an intraday high of 2731 before closing at 2704, up 3 points. The Dow opened at 24855, reached an intraday high of 25157 before closing at 24962, up 162. The Nas has been on somewhat of a winning streak. It opened at 7252 and rose to an intraday high of 7281 before closing at 7210, down 8 points. To date it is the only index to remain well above its 62% retracement value of 7173. The VIX is showing signs of returning to a less than 20 value.

It is hurry up and wait time for anyone with the expectation of a retest of the early February lows. I have an app called Webull that I watch throughout the day. One of the things I like about it is that it is the only I've seen that shows net cashflow in and out of the NYSE and Nasdaq. Cash is starting to move slowly back into the NYSE now. The Nas has seen positive cash for about a week.

2/23/18

Futures were pretty much the same and as before, the indices all jumped higher as the morning progressed. The difference today was that the majors maintained the runup right to the closing bells. Somewhat reminiscent of Jan. 26, before all hell broke loose. One of the contributors for StockCharts.com is looking for a resolution this coming week as to the direction of the markets. I would like to see a retest this coming week as well because there are no technicals that point to a continuation of the bull market at present.

The S&P opened at 2716 and reached a high of 2748 closing at 2747, up 43 points. The closing value was four points above the 62% retracement for the first time. The Dow opened at 25051 and reached a high of 25314 before closing at 25304, up 348 points. It remains below the 62% retracement level of 25379, the only major to do so now that the S&P closed above its value. The Nas opened at 7261 and rose to 7338 before closing at 7337, up 127 points. It is still below its recent high of 7506 but could close on it this coming week.

There was a headline from the WSJ regarding personal borrowing for purposes of investing in the stock market and the impact it could have, especially for those using margin. When margin calls start hitting it only forces drops in share prices and consequently the entire market.

As I write this I am looking forward to this coming week. My personal hope is a retest, but time will tell.

2/26/18

Monday was a mixed feelings day. I have been pretty certain that we would start to see the start toward a retest of the prior early February lows. But that was not the case. The S&P opened at 2757 achieved an intraday high of 2781 and closed at 2780. The Dow opened at 25403 reaching a high of 25733 and closed at 25709, up 399 on the day. The Nas opened at 7373 reaching 7422 and closed there, up 84 points.

I have no reason to feel comfortable about moving out of the PLUS fund based upon the available T/A that I created or from StockCharts.com charts and blogs. I also didn't realize how often I was trading in funds since November until I prepared a spreadsheet with the details. For that reason alone, I am cautious about making any new commitments to equity funds.

2/27/18

The S&P opened at 2780 reaching a high of 2789 before reversing through the rest of the day to 2744 where it closed, down 36. The Dow opened at 25736 and reached an intraday high of 25800 before reversing direction to close at 25410, down 299. The Nas opened at 7416 rising to 7438 and closed at 7330, down 91 points on the day. This change in direction was something I have hoped for because my expectation is for a retest of the 2533 February low so that I can consider going positive in order to recoup prior losses. As with yesterday, there is nothing happening technically to make me comfortable with investing. So now it is a waiting game. Worthy of note has been the fact that the volumes during the recent market increases has been lower than the most recent few days. Cash in/out for the NYSE and NASDAQ has been negative.

2/28/18

Well, the month ended in much the same way that it began…. Down! But For me I'm comfortable because I am expecting a retest of the Feb. 9 intraday lows. As a reminder the S&P was at 2533, the Dow 23360 and the Nas. 6630.

The S&P opened at 2754 enjoying a brief high of 2761 before closing at 2714, down 30 and below its 50-day simple moving average. The Dow performed in basically the same manner opening at 25485 and reaching a high of 25576 before closing at 25029, down 381 points. The Nas opened at 7371 achieving a high of 7387 before dropping 57 points to close at 7273. So, for my purposes the indices are now doing what my expectations have been since the bounce after Feb. 9. As before, there is nothing positive in any of the StockCharts.com or my own charts. So, time for more patience.

March

3/01/18

Some more confirmation that the indices will be testing previous lows with today's closes. The S&P opened at 2715 and reached a high of 2731 before heading south, closing at its low for the day of 2678, down 36 points from Wednesday. The Dow fared no better opening at 25024 and reaching an intraday high of 25185 before closing at 24609, down 420. It had been as low as 24443, down 586 intraday. The Nas opened at 7275 and hit an intraday high of 7308 and a low of 7118 (-190 spread) before closing at 7181, down 92. Volumes have been on the high side for the last few days helping to give me more confidence that a retest is more likely than not. Time will tell of course.

3/02/18

The indices are seemingly in agreement that the markets are in correction mode. The Dow was down again today but the Nas and S&P were positive, but on below normal volumes. The S&P opened at 2659 and reached a high of 2696 (up 20 from Thursday's close) before closing at 2692, up 14 points. The Dow opened at 24395 reaching a high of 24592 before closing at 24538 down 71. The spread was 374 points throughout the day. The Nas opened at 7099 reaching a high of 7267 and closing at 7258, up 77. Like the Dow, the Nas ranged quite a bit between 7085 and 7267 (182 points). These moves serve to indicate just how emotional traders are during uncertain times like we have been experiencing for the last month.

As has been the case for several weeks now, there are no positive signals for a resumption of the prior bull market. So, I continue to wait.

3/05 – 07/2018.

The biggest threat to the market came Tuesday with the news that Gary Cohn was leaving the White House.

The S&P opened Monday at 2681 and closed yesterday at 2727, up 46 points (1,7%) over the three days. The Dow opened at 24471 and closed yesterday at 24801, up 330 points or 1.3%. The Nas opened at 7223 on Monday and closed at 7397 on Wednesday, up 174 or 2.5%. It is starting to look like there may not be a retest of the February lows. I see slight improvements in the technicals, especially when reviewing the indices MACD and PMO signals that are not yet bullish but have at least changed to a more favorable direction. Time will tell. Wednesday was the first day that the 20-day moving average for bullish T/A was higher than the bearish T/A since February 2. Not so yet with the P&F but the ratio is improving.

3/08/18

The market is beginning to behave in a more customary fashion. The daily spreads between the high and low for the indices is more rational and returning to the daily movements prior to the correction. The charts that I maintain are reinforcing this and most are moving into the old trading range prior to the unsustainable January jumps of 4%.

The S&P opened at 2733 and reached a high of 2740, closing at 2739, up 12 points on much more normal volume. The Dow opened at 24853 and reached an intraday high of 24950 before closing at 24895, up 94. The Nas opened at 7423 and hit an intraday high of 7435 before closing at 7428, up 31.

The all-important VIX was below 16.5 at the COB, helping to foster more logical trading activity.

3/09/18

Today saw a stellar performance in the market. The S&P opened at 2753, gapping up 14 points from Thursday's close. This index reached a high of 2787 closing at its high for the day, up 48. Not to be outdone, the Dow opened at 25005 also gapping up 110 points before closing at 25336, up 441 points on the day. The Nas opened at 7476 and gapped up as well. It closed at 7561, up 133 for the day. This was a new 52 week high for the Nasdaq.

The previous all-time high for the S&P was 2872. This index is 85 points below that and it's not unreasonable to expect that this ground could be covered by next week, IMO. As mentioned yesterday my charts reflect a favorable T/A 20 day moving average. But we are still lagging as regards the P&F moving average although it is improving slowly. Until it is at least 1:1, I'm not committing more PLUS funds to other risk funds unless the S&P reaches a new high.

3/12/18

Things got off to a roaring start with the market opening before settling down by the end of the day.

The S&P opened at 2791 and closed at 2783, down 4 points from Friday's close. The Dow opened at 25372 and reached a high of 25449 before closing at 25179, down 157. The Nas opened at 7581 and closed at 7588, up 27 points. This index reached an intraday high of 7609, an all-time high. As for the charts there was nothing new.

3/13/18

Today was a down day across all indices and for the present indicative of a breather, given how healthy the recent recovery from February's lows. The S&P opened at 2792 hitting an intraday high of 2802 (up 19) before closing at 2765, down 18. The Dow opened at 25258 achieving an early morning high of 25376 (up 197) before closing at 25007, down 172. The Nas opened at 7628 reached a high of 7637 before closing at 7511, down 77.

Noteworthy was the fact that bullish P&F summary exceeded the bearish summary. This was the first time since February 2, although the 20-day SMA has a way to go.

3/14/18

Pi Day…and the VIX isn't representative having risen to 17.24 over the last two days, closing above its 50-day moving average.

The S&P was out of the gate opening at 2774 and reaching 2777 (+12) before closing at 2749, down 16 points. Not wanting to feel left out, the Dow opened higher at 25087 and reached 25130 (+123) before reaching a low of 24668, recovering somewhat to close at 24758, down 249 points. The spread was 461 points during the day or 1.8%. Sure, signs that volatility remains a big issue to traders. The Nas opened at 7540 and closed at 7497, down 14. It is now 140 points down from its intraday high of 7637 reached just yesterday.

The Dow is having an issue with remaining above its 50-day moving average after closing above it twice now since February 2, only to close below it again today. The S&P remained ever so slightly above it at the close. It doesn't bode well that these two indices are having issues here. Just glad I am 2/3 cash.

3/15/18

No great calamities although the indices were pretty much down with the exception of the Dow. The VIX was down slightly.

The S&P opened at 2754 rising to 2763 before losing steam to close at 2747, down 2. The Dow opened at 24837 and reached an intraday high of 25054 before closing at 24873, up 116. The Nas opened at 7509 and reached an intraday high of 7525 before closing at 7482, down 15 points.

Nothing to get excited about on any charts. I did close out minor amounts in my 401 funds and hopefully put them to work in a REIT fund that is one of the few with a positive daily PMO.

3/16/18

The major indices closed higher although not excitedly so. It was a triple witching day, so nothing in terms of any future clarity. The S&P opened at 2751 and ranged as high as 2762 before closing at 2752, up 5. The Dow opened at 24877 and was as high as 25031 intraday. It closed at 24947, up 73. The Nas opened at 7504 and reached 7514 before closing at 7482. Today was the first day since last Friday that these indices all closed higher albeit in the case of the Nas we are talking a whopping $.25 higher close.

Technically speaking the indices can go either way as the Dow is forming a symmetrical triangle and the

S&P looks to have done the same. The StockCharts.com folks are not in agreement as to where we go from here either, based on T/A results. It is safe to say that no one is highly bullish though and only a couple who are more bearish than bullish. Time will tell, especially after the FED meeting this coming week with the anticipated rise in rates.

3/19/18

Today was kind of a wild one on Wall Street. The indices all opened down, the Nas being especially hard hit. The S&P opened at 2741 and saw an intraday low of 2695 before recovering to 2713, down 39. It was down as much as 57 points intraday. The Dow opened at 24894 and reached an intraday low of 24453 (-494) before recovering to 24611, down 336 points. The Nas opened at 7419 and reached 7285 (-197) before closing at 7344, down 138 from Friday. If any index needed a correction it was the Nas which has done well since recovering two weeks ago from its Feb. 9 low of 6631.

The VIX was as high as 22 today before settling back to 19, closing above its 50 Day SMA. The Dow remains 3% below its 50 Day SMA and the S&P closed below its 50 Day SMA for the first time in seven days. Its PMO remains positive.

3/20/18

The S&P opened at 2715 and reached 2724 before closing at 2717, up 4 for the day. The Dow opened at 24651 and reached an intraday high of 24804 but closed at 24727, up 116. It had been up 193 earlier in the day. The Nas opened at 7353 and reached a high of 7381 before closing at 7364, up 20 points. Truly lackluster as the indices continue basically moving sideways.

3/21/18

The S&P opened at 2715 the same as Tuesday and reached a high of 2739 before reversing direction to close at 2712, down 5 points. The Dow at 24723 reaching a high of 24978 before also closing down at 24682 (-45). The Nas opened at 7348 and had an intraday high of 6416 before closing at 7345, down 19 points. Facebook and other social media sites have been responsible for the recent fallout in this index.

The FED announced a 25 basis point rise today as expected but there seems to be a good deal of concern on the tariff issue announced a few days ago by the Administration. We need to see what happens going forward.

3/22/18

No complacency today!

Overnight already wasn't boding well for today as the majors were all down in a big way. The S&P opened at 2691 and reached 2642 late in the day to close at 2644, down 68 points (-2.52%). The Dow opened at 24526 and reached a low of 23939before closing at 23958, down 724 points (-2.93%). The Nas opened at 7258 and saw a low of 7164 before closing at 7169, down 179 points (-2.43%).

Matt was in touch which always happens on busy days like this as of late and which I enjoy. He is 95% cash whereas I'm at 50%. I am satisfied with the funds I am in but would like the chance to get aggressive when the charts favor it. The VIX is up to 23.35, and well above its 50-day MA. The PMO looks ready to cross above the signal line but I'm believing it ain't going to happen. I told Matt I want to see it below 17 before I move into other funds. I am also waiting for the S&P to move to 2620-2635 to see some stabilization and as of today the 200-day MA is 2584, the next support. The double bottom would occur at 2533. Tomorrow should give some guidance.

3/22/18

The good news. The S&P did bounce off its 200 Day SMA if only slightly. The Dow and Nas were down strongly as well. Horrible day for equities. A terrible week as well.

The S&P opened down again at 2647 and reached a low of 2586 (-58) before closing at 2588, down 55 points. The Dow opened at 23995 and reached an intraday low of 23506, (-449) before closing at 23533, down 425 points. The Nas opened at 7171 and reached an intraday low of 6993 (-176) where it closed. For the week the S&P was down 164 points, the Dow down 1414 points and the Nas was down 489 points. The S&P managed to find support at its 200 Day SMA. The Feb. 9 intraday low was 2533. Friday's close was just 55 points above that. The Dow suffered an intraday low of 23360 on that date, so closed 173 points above it. The Nas is in somewhat better territory closing 363 points above the 6630 intraday low of Feb. 9.

So, best guess? Until Facebook settles at some lower value the Nas and S&P will continue lower unless there is renewed strength in other equities in the indices. I can see the three indices retesting the Feb. 9 lows sometime this week.

3/26/18

Beginning of uptrend or dead cat bounces?

Quite a jump in the indices on Monday with major advances. The S&P opened up at 2619 and closed at 2659, up 70 points. The Dow opened up at 23826 and closed at 24203, up 669. The Nas opened at 7125 and closed at 7229, up 228 points. With such increases I would have expected much higher volumes than what we saw yesterday which would make a strong argument that these upward moves were dead cat bounces. Anyway, I'm going to stay pat with our current funds unless something technically positive happens.

3/27/18

Looks like it was a dead cat bounce yesterday!

The majors were down again, and I doubt that many traders were surprised after yesterday's drama.

The S&P opened at 2668 and reached an intraday high of 2674 before reversing course to close at 2613, down 46. It had been down 62 points near the end of the day before recovering some. The Dow opened up at 24277 and reached an intraday high of 24446 (+243) before catching the ill wind and closing down 345 points at 23856. It reached an intraday low of 23709. Swings of 500 points or more are becoming common now. The Nas opened at 7255, it's high before closing at 7008, down 212 points. It was down 256 points at its intraday low. FB and chip stocks drove stocks lower.

Hard to tell what will happen day to day especially with a high VIX that reached 24 but dropped to 22.53 at the close.

Patience is the name of the game.

3/28/18

Different day same results except it was choppy.

The S&P opened at 2611 and reached an intraday high of 2632 before closing at 2605, down 8. The Dow opened at 23883 and reached a high of 24092 before closing at 23848, down 9 points. It had reached an intraday low of 23729. The spread was 363 points so some improvement. The Nas is still on a down slope opening at 6978 and reaching an intraday low of 6901 before losing at 6949, down 60 points.

One could look at the choppy movement as a positive. It might indicate that this correction is trying to complete its move and trying to find support. Time will tell.

Thursday is the last trading day of March because of Good Friday. Maybe April and Qtrly earnings can see the indices turn positive.

3/29/18

Based upon the activity yesterday I am believing that the bottom is in.

The S&P opened at 2614 and reached an intraday high of 2659 in the afternoon. After opening, the index reached a low of 2610 before moving higher. The intraday spread was 49 points. The index closed at 2641, up 36. Based on volume and the morning characteristics it appears to me that the selling has run out of steam. The Dow opened at 23949 and bottomed at 23928 before rising to an intraday high of 24314 (+466), closing at 24103, up 255. As with the S&P it appeared that the selling after the markets opened quickly subsided and that buyers were calling the shots for most of the day. Cash was positive for the NYSE all day for a change. The Nas opened at 6985 dropping to 6936 and then put in an intraday high of 7120 before closing at 7063, up 114 on the day. Cash was negative in early trading and then positive for the rest of the day. The VIX dropped throughout the day closing at 19.97, another favorable factor to end the day, month and quarter because the markets are closed on Good Friday.

April

4/02/18

What a way to start the week, month and quarter! Maybe the bottom isn't in yet. Or maybe this was the blow off before the market goes higher. Time for more patience.

The S&P was down from the start, opening at 2633, down 8. It reached an intraday low of 2554 (-87) before recovering somewhat to close at 2582, down 59 points. The Dow opened down 26 points and reached an intraday low of 23345 (-758) before recovering to 23644, down 459 points. The Nas followed suit by opening down 47 to 7016. It reached an intraday low of 6806 (-257) before recovering to close at 6870, down 193. The VIX closed at 23.57 but had been as high as 25.72. The S&P closed below its 200 Day SMA. The Dow dropped below its 200 Day SMA but closed above it. The Nas alone left the 200 Day SMA flirting for another day.

My bad saying that the bottom was in on last Thursday!

4/03/18

Two steps backward, one step forward – or has the market settled down? Today was positive for the market with about a 70% recovery from yesterday's losses. The indices opened up with the Dow remaining positive while the S&P and Nas were briefly in the red. The S&P opened at 2592 and reached a high of 2619 before closing at 2614, up 33 on the day. The Dow opened at 23698 and reached an intraday high of 24044 before closing at 24033, up 389. The Nas opened at 6924 and reached an intraday low of 6834 (-35) before turning higher to close at 6941, up 71 points. So that's 2 out of 3 days with positive closes since last Thursday. The VIX is still high at 21.23 but down from 23.57. It still remains above its 50-day SMA which is now 19.39 and rising.

Matthew texted to say he put funds in the market yesterday.

4/04/05

Out of the woods yet? Not 100% sure yet but today was very telling. The indices were all well below water overnight and it only got worse at the opening bell. The S&P opened at 2584, down 30 from the

prior close. It hit a low of 2574 before coming up for air to close at 2645, up 30. The Dow opened at 23654, down 379 and like the S&P struggled most of the day before moving above the prior close to end at 24264, up 231. The Nas opened at 6812, down 129 but managed a healthy close of 7042, up 101. So, it is now 3 out of 4 days that the close has been positive going back to March 29. The VIX closed at 20.06, down 1.04. It reached 24.51 in the morning before settling down and is in reach of its 50-day SMA which is a good thing.

4/05/18

Now we are up to 4 out of five days with positive closes and that's a big improvement from the prior weeks. The only issue was that the indices didn't close near the highs. Hopefully it was because of profit taking.

The S&P opened at 2657, up 13 and reached 2672 intraday. It closed at 2663, up 18. The Dow opened at 24314, up 50, and reached a high of 24622, closing at 24505, up 241. The Nas opened at 7099, up 57 and was at 7112 intraday before closing at 7077 up 34. The VIX ended the day at 18.88, down 1.18 and closing below its 50-day SMA for the first time since Mar. 16.

4/06/18

It was too much to ask to go 5 out of 6! The indices closed the week by getting clobbered. Not really much of a surprise given yesterday's action in the afternoon but the selloff on a percentage basis was. The S&P opened down at 2646, down 17. It reached an intraday low of 2586 (-77) before recovering somewhat at the close, down 58 at 2604. It remained above its 200-day SMA albeit breaching it briefly intraday. The Dow opened down 131 points at 24734. It was downhill from there to an intraday low of 23738 (-767) before closing at 23933, down 572. The Nas opened at 7000, down 77 and achieved a low of 6878 (-198) before recovering to 6915, down 161 points. The VIX rose to 21.48, above its 50-day SMA once again. The DOW and Nasdaq remained above the respective 200-day SMA for each index. All three indices closed below last week's closing averages.

4/09/18

If you periodically check the indices throughout the day like I do, then you have to be disheartened to see the trending up through most of the day only to see it go downhill by the EOD. This happened today. To my knowledge there was no negative news that the markets had to deal with. It is especially annoying given that the futures all opened higher.

The S&P opened at 2617, up 13 points from Friday. The index reached an intraday high of 2654, (+50) before plummeting to 2613, up 9 points. The close compared to the opening price is getting to be a habit of late. The Dow opened at 24038, up 105 and reached a high of 24373 intraday, (+440) before falling to 23979, up 46. The Nas opened at 6971, up 56 and reached an intraday high of 7075, (+159) before dropping to 6950, up 35 from Friday.

Because earnings season will soon be upon us, I would be expecting marked improvement in the coming days. If not, it will confirm a bear market rather than a correction, IMO.

Well, in retrospect, I guess the raid by the FBI on Trump's attorney caused the market decline in the afternoon.

4/10/18

Unlike yesterday there were no last-minute surprises to scare off traders. The indices all closed near intraday highs. The S&P opened up at 2638, up 25 before reaching an intraday high of 2665 (+52) before closing at 2657 up 44. The Dow opened at 24199 up 220, reached an intraday high of 24511 (+532), and closed at 24408, up 429. Likewise, the Nas also opened up at 7061, up 111, and reached an intraday high of 7118 (+168) before settling at 7094, up 144 on the day. Because of the prior two months this is a welcomed advance but there are hurdles to jump before I can get comfortable with being fully invested.

4/11/18

Inflation fears expressed by the FED was the supposed cause of today's drops across the board. Each index opened lower and seesawed the rest of the session. The S&P opened down at 2644 (-13) and managed in intraday low of 2639 and a high of 2661 before settling at 2642, down 15. The Dow opened at 24274, down 134 from the previous day. The intraday low was 24151 and the high 24367. It closed down 219 points to 24189. The Nas opened at 7055, down 39. It hit an intraday low of 7055 and a high of 7129 before closing at 7069, down 25 on the day. The S&P and Nas were positive during the day at one point. One positive highlight is that my daily chart results of T/A and P&F sums has been over 1 for two days in a row. Last time that happened was on 3/!3.

Inflation isn't newsworthy enough to explain the down day because we have been hearing about it since December, based on the rates of employment and a somewhat steady but slight increase in wages and some consumer prices. Part of me says that the market makers are at rest for now as they prepare for the earnings season that should stimulate more buying. We'll see!

4/12/18

We closed higher again today but well below the day's intraday highs. The S&P opened at 2654, up 12 and reached an intraday high of 2675 (+33) before moving down to close at 2664, up 22. It closed above the midpoint of its Bollinger bands for the first time since a month ago for what it's worth. The Dow finished at 24483, up 294 but well off its high of 24592 (+403). The Nas opened at 7112, up 43 and reached an intraday high of 7166 (+97) before closing at 7140, up by 71. Earnings season is upon us, so I would expect higher movement across the board for at least the rest of the week. Of course, this could be countered with a geopolitical or earnings surprise. The market corrected knowing that there were high expectations for 1st quarter earnings. It would be very bearish to see those expectations not being met. With today's closes my T/A and P&F sums were again over 1. That's now three consecutive days.

4/13/18

All in all, it wasn't a bad week for the markets and better than most for the last two and a half months. The S&P closed at 2656, down 8 for the day but up 52 for the week. It opened up 13 and reached an intraday high of 2680 before sliding to the close. The Dow gained 427 for the week although it lost 123 today closing at 24360. The Nas also had a good week gaining 192. The index closed down today 34 points to end at 7107.

Interesting was the fact that the first quarter earnings reported by the banks was higher than expected but still sold off throughout the day. Many more reports to come though within the next few weeks. The VIX closed at 17.41. Nice direction for a change and below its 50-day MA. It is below its PMO and

PPO are below the signal lines. For the fourth day in a row my T/A P&F sums are above 1. The last 4-day streak was Mar. 8 thru Mar 13. (weekend in there).

4/16/18

Because we owed, I waited until today to e-file our taxes. That's that for another year. As for the markets they did well today. The S&P opened higher at 2670, up 14. It reached a high of 2686 and just kissed the 50-day MA before retreating to close at 2678, up 22 on the day. The Dow opened at 24483, up 123. It's high was 24675, up 315 and fell back to 24573, up 213. The index was briefly above its 50-day MA before retreating. The Nas opened up at 7154, up 47. It reached an intraday high of 7179 (+72) before retreating to 7156, up 50 points. It too remained below its 50-day MA.

The VIX closed at 16.43 and well below its 50-day MA. Five days now for my T/A P&F sums to remain above 1. Last time was January 26. The T/A side is carrying the water. Have a way to go before the P&F turns positive.

It concerns me a little that the indices don't hold the intraday highs. I would be much more comfortable if they all close well above respective 50-day MAs. Maybe in the next day or two.

4/17/18

Good day all around. To start with the indices cleared 50-day MA across the board and closed near the highs for the day after opening above the prior closes. The S&P opened at 2693, up 15 and reached an intraday high of 2713 before closing at 2707, up 29. The Dow opened at 24682, up 109 and reached an intraday high of 24859 (+286) before closing at 24787, up 214. The Nas opened up 7215, up 59 and reached a high of 7299, up 143 before closing at 7281, up 125 on the day. The VIX closed down at 15.27 and had been below 15 at one point in the day. This trend was great news as well.

Now at day six of consecutive T/A and P&F sums above 1. In fact, today it was above 2 for the first time since January 23. And fir the first time since March 13 the sum of the bullish P&F values was higher than the negative if only by 2. PPOs and PMOs are all favorable on the daily charts as well. I will consider investing more now that the 50-day MAs have been eclipsed.

4/18/18

Today was a good day in every respect because it seemed like a normal trading day for a change. There was no drama. The indices did nothing spectacular. The S&P opened slightly up at 2710 and reached a high of 2717 before closing at 2709, up 2. The Dow opened at 24821 up 35 and reached an intraday high of 24833 (+46) before closing at 24748, down 39. The Nas opened at 7292 and closed up at 7295, up 14. In addition, the VIX rose to 15.6, up slightly but still something I can feel comfortable with. The T/A and P&F sums were again above 1. This is the consistency that is needed to instill comfort. It is now two days in a row that the P&F bulls sum was higher than the bears sum.

4/19/18

The indices have temporarily run out of steam which is a good thing given the nice run of the last several days. The S&P opened down at 2701 and hit an intraday low of 2682 before recovering to 2693, down 16 on the day. The Dow opened at 24711 and was as low as 24557 (-191) before recovering to close at 24665, down 83. The Nas opened down at 7259, down 36 and reached an intraday low of 7215 (-80) before closing at 7238, down 57 on the day. The VIX rose .47 to close at 16.07. It is still in my comfort range for now. The T/A and P&F sums continue to remain above 1.

4/20/18

Today was not a fun day. The indices were all pegged to open lower and did. Problem was that they didn't finish the day anywhere above the 50-day MA. All three closed below them after moving above on Tuesday. One can argue that this was to fill the gaps created when the markets opened up on Tuesday, but they did that and more. I could also argue that the recent few days of gains simply filled the gaps created in mid-March when the indices gapped down.

The S&P opened down a ½ point and spent the rest of the day heading south to 2661 (-32) before closing at 2670, down 23. The Dow opened down slightly as well at 24657. It too forgot where north was and hit 24375 (-290) before closing at 24463, down 202. The Nas opened at 7221, down 17, then followed through with the other indices to a mid-day low of 7123 (-115) before closing at 7146, down 92. The T/A and P&F sums dropped below 1 for the first time in nine days ago. Another issue to watch out for is an article on StockCharts.com regarding a possible right shoulder forming to complete a four- year head and shoulders pattern. If it completes the pattern it forecasts a breakdown in bond prices and increases in yields. If this happens there would be an expectation for equity prices to fall as well as traders head for the higher yields. Next week's action will tell the tale of the tape. The indices need to move up and over their 50-day averages or it will probably be best to get out of equities and see where the lower prices settle. I'm glad I didn't move more from the PLUS fund.

4/23/18

Today ended pretty much as it began with only slight changes from Friday. The S&P opened up 5 points and hit extremes of 2658 for the low (-12) and a high of 2683

(+13) before closing at 2670. The Dow opened up 25 points and reaches an intraday high of 24537 (+74) and a low of 24329 (-134) before closing at 24449, down 14. The Nas opened at 7174, up 28. It reached an intraday high of 7196 (+50) and a low of 7094 (-52) but closed at 7129, down 18. With this type of activity, little movement at the close, I'm guessing that we are in a period of accumulation. This is the biggest earnings reporting week, so I would have expected higher closes than the last two trading days. As for the sums of the T/A and P&F, it is back over 1 but slightly so.

4/24/18

What the hell! Earnings reports coming out are great but as one of the StockCharts.com guys asked, "Has your portfolio ever been run over by a Caterpillar?" Reason being is that Cat and others are all reporting great quarters but express that a little slow down might be on tap next quarter and inflation costs might start eating into future earnings. Anyway, the markets all ran for the hills.

The S&P opened at 2681, up 11 and reached a high of 2684 before getting on the express slide and falling to 2617 (-53) before recovering somewhat to close at 2635, down 36. The Dow opened up at 24580, up 131 before falling to a low of 23829 (-620). It closed at 24024, down 425. The Nas opened at 7161, up 32 and hit an intraday low of 6962 (-166) before recovering to 7007, down 122. So, a great earnings day but negative on the major indices.

Maybe some are running scared because the 10-year yield rose above 3% for the first time in four years. There is always an explanation when the market reality doesn't make any sense. The sums went below 1 today as well.

4/25/18

Nuth'in to write home about but the S&P and Dow closed in the green today. The S&P opened at 2635

and closed at 2639, up 5. Nothing dramatic regarding intraday activity. The Dow opened at 24070, up 46 and hit a low of 23823 (-201) and a high of 24146 before closing at 24084, up 60 points. The Nas finished in the red at 7004, down 4. It had an intraday low of 6927 (-80) and a high of 7031. The T/A and P&F sums closed below 1 for the second day in a row. The VIX is still high at 17.85 down slightly after being as high as 19.84. It remains below its 50 Day SMA although above it for a short stint.

4/26/18

The indices opened higher and closed with nice gains. The problem I had is that we witness movement up throughout the day with good sell-off at day's end. This is basically the recent pattern and it's not comforting.

The S&P opened up at 2652 (+13), reaching a high of 2676 (+37) before closing at 2667, up 28 on the day. The Dow opened at 24129 (+45), reached an intraday high of 24402 (+318) before closing at 24322 for a 239 higher close. The Nas also opened higher at 7080 (+76) and reached an intraday high of 7143 (+140) before closing at 7119, up 115.

The pattern of trading is the same as in the past several weeks where the jumpers start at about 3:15 after healthy advances throughout the day. This activity has been followed by drops to or through the 200 Day SMA but closing above it. The indices were all over their 50 Day SMA a week ago but simply didn't have the stamina to sustain a rising market. All of this activity is going on in spite of record earnings.

4/27/18

Not much movement today. I had expected more given that it was the end of the biggest earnings report weeks and near the end of the month.

The S&P opened at 2675, up 8 and reached an intraday high of 2677 and a low of 2659 before settling at 2670, up 3. The Dow opened at 24342 up 20 and managed a high of 24359 and a low of 24194 (-128).

It closed at 24311 losing 11 on the day. The Nas opened at 7196, up 77, reaching an intraday high of 7197 and low of 7084, down 35. It managed to close at 7120, up 1. The indices all remain below their 50 Day SMA. I am beginning to wonder if the lows on Feb. 9 the creation of an inverse H&S formation and we have yet to see some even lower lows to form a head. Of course, if this bears fruit it will be bullish and a good time to get back in. There is simply no excitement and there is still a daily run on cash at the NYSE. That needs to end as well. THE VIX did close at 15.41, which put it at support. The 200 Day SMA is rising and that should make it easier for the VIX to drop below it. I'll believe it when I see it.

4/30/18

Another day of consolidation. Still hoping that's all it is anyway. Over the weekend I traded out of the T Rowe Price fund into the Investco Dividend fund. Should be safe and the chart looks good for it.

The S&P opened up at 2675 (+5) and reached an intraday high of 2683 before falling to 2648 down 22. The Dow left the gate at 24410, up 99 and reached an intraday high of 24498 (+187) before trailing off to 24163, down 148. The Nas started up at 7134, up 14 and reached an intraday high of 7169 (+49) before closing down at 7066, down 54 on the day. The indices all closed at session lows. One geopolitical event was the Israeli announcement that Iran has been lying about following the Obama era agreement that paid millions to Iran in return for Its promise to refrain from a nuclear weapons program. The Israelis have all of the related documentation, somehow confiscated by stealth.

This news could account for the selling today, but I think it is attributable to the ongoing uncertainty of

almost everything. The VIX is at 16.04 and cash was pretty much negative again on the NYSE all day and the NASDAQ went negative late morning.

May

5/01/18

The S&P and Nas closed up by day's end. Given that all the indices were basically oversold it shouldn't be a surprise and there was nothing in the way of news to influence the market. I was surprised to watch the VIX fall by close of business as well closing at 15.49.

The S&P opened at 2644 (-4) and reached an intraday low of 2625, down 23, before rising through the afternoon to close up 7 at 2655. The Dow opened at 24117, down 46, and reached an intraday low of 23808 (-355) before recovering to 24099, down 64. The Nas opened down at 7054 (-12) and reached an intraday low of 7036 (-30) before turning the corner to close at 7131, up 64. Cash was negative throughout most of the day on the NAS and NYSE both. It was slightly positive only in the last 30 minutes or so.

I have no expectations yet because there are still negative "vibes" with the T/A and P&F summations.

5/02/18

The temperature registered 90 degrees today, so I was outside for a good part of it. There was nothing new in the markets, so I'll just give highlights about the continuing consolidation. The S&P was as high as 2661 before turning tail to close at 2636, down 19. The Dow was at 24186 intraday before closing down 174 points to 23925. The Nas rose to 7169 before closing at 7101, down 30. I thought the VIX was going to close below 15 but not yet. Until the indices hit new lows or breakout over the 50 Day SMAs it is best for me to do nothing.

5/03/18

Still trying to find a direction. The S&P swung wildly again, opening at 2628 (-8) and reaching a low of 2595, down 41 before recovering to close at 2630, down 6. The Dow reached an intraday low of 23531 (-394) before managing a close of 23930, up 5. The Nas opened down as well and was at 6991 (-110) before closing at 7088, down only 13. Needless to say, the volatility index was active as well reaching 18.66 before closing at 15.96.

5/04/18

Good end of the week with slight losses for the S&P and Dow and a gain for the Nas since last Friday. The day opened looking like it was going to be a downer, again, with the S&P opening at 2621 (-8) and reached an intraday low early of 2615. The rest of the day was positive with the index closing at 2663, up 34. It had been up 41. The Dow opened at 23865, down 65 and hit an intraday low of 23779 (-151) before cruising higher the rest of the session. It closed at 24263, up 332. The Nas opened at 7066 (-22), reaching a low of 7058 (-30) before gaining 121 points to close at 7210.

More importantly, the VIX hit an intraday low of 10.91 before closing at 14.73. Let's hope it remains below 15 in the future. Important too was the positive cash all day long for both the Nas and NYSE. For the first time in a while it remained positive all day for both exchanges. It would be wonderful to see this continue. For the first time all week the T/A and P&F sums were over 1 as well.

Not saying we are out of the woods, but I did put $25K in the S&P fund this morning after seeing the quick turn of events with the markets going higher, the cash being positive and the VIX taking the sharp drop. Monday will tell us what next to expect. It is important to note that the S&P has hit or penetrated its 200 Day SMA eight times since the first of April, twice in the last two days, and closed above it seven of them to include the last two days.

5/07/18

It would be hard to beat Friday's gains but today was okay. The S&P opened at 2669, up 6. It reached an intraday high of 2683 (+20) before closing at 2673, up 9. The Dow reached an intraday high of 24479 (+216) before closing at 24357, up 95. The Nas opened up at 7242 (+81) before closing at 7265, up 56. It closed above its 50 Day SMA, the only major index to do so. The VIX closed at 14.72. It was over 15 for part of the day. The S&P and Dow were above the respective 50 Day SMAs during the session. My hope is that it closes above them during this week.

5/08/18

It is hard to say for sure which way the markets are leaning but they are definitely trying to choose. The S&P opened at 2670, down 3 and hit an intraday low of 2655 (-18) before recovering to close at 2672, down 1. The Dow opened slightly down before advancing to 24414 (+57) and then declined to 24198 (-159). It recovered throughout the afternoon to close up 3 at 24360. The Nas opened down 10 points at 7255 and ran red all day after being up briefly at 7278. Its intraday low was 7224, down 41. It too recovered to close at 7267, up 2. The VIX closed at 14.71.

5/09/18

Good news day for a change. After a slow start to the morning the indices took off. The S&P opened at 2678 up 6 and hit an intraday high of 2701 before closing at 2698, up 26. It broke up above the triangle that had been forming and closed above its 50 Day SMA for the first time in a month. The Dow opened at 24399 and reached an intraday high of 24586 before closing at 24543, up 182. The Dow also closed above its 50 Day SMA for the first time since mid-April. The Nas opened up at 7281 and reached an intraday high of 7345 before closing at 7340, up 73. It remained above its 50 Day SMA for the fourth day in a row. Also positive on the day was the VIX close at 13.42 and closed below its 200 Day SMA for the first since around Jan. 25/26. So, you gotta love today's closing results. Let's hope it wasn't a head fake.

5/10/18

Another good day for the markets. The S&P started at 2705, up 7 from yesterday. It continued up through the remainder of the day to close at 2723, up 25. It closed above the mid-April high of 2717, an important T/A factor. The Dow opened up 49 to 24592. It hit an intraday high of 24795 (+252) before retreating somewhat to close at 24740, up 197. The Nas opened at 7356, up 11 and hit an intraday high of 7414, up 74 before closing at a respectable 7405, up 65. It goes without saying that this index has been in the leadership position. I have a concern that there has not been much of a volume jump with the latest price increases. The flip side though is that the VIX continues to drop and is now at 13.23 and that it closed below its 200 Day SMA for the second day in a row.

5/11/18

Today was an especially good one because it was a Friday and except for the Nas the indices ended up. No drama, no notable intraday highs or lows. It was for all intents and purposes a normal Friday trading day for a change!

The S&P opened basically at yesterday's close and hit an intraday low of 2717 and a high of 2733 before closing at 2723, up 5. The Dow opened at 24758 and hit an intraday low of 24717 and a high of 24869 before closing at 24831, up a respectable 92. The Nas lost ground closing at 7403, down 2. This was all in all a very respectable week.

The VIX closed at 12.65. This is quite a change from the last three months and at a very comfortable level. It's certainly something I can live with. On top of that the indices are all above their 50 Day SMA. The markets seem to be more focused now that the president has told Iran to pound sand with regard to the previous administration's "caving". Oil has remained above $70 which is acceptable for now.

As for my T/A and P&F daily sums, they've also turned positive for both summations. Can't complain! It was a good week and although there are resistance levels ahead, I think that the indices have finally started to favor the bulls for a change.

5/14/18

The pace of the market is good and more in line with accumulation. The S&P opened up 5 at 2733 and hit 2740 intraday (+14) before closing at 2730, up 2. The Dow opened up 48 at 24879. It reached an intraday high of 24994 (+163) before closing at 24899, up 68. The Nas opened up 27 at 7429. It reached an intraday high of 7458 (+56) before almost closing in the red. It eked out a gain of 8 in the final trading minutes as did the S&P. The VIX closed at 12.93, up marginally.

There was enough geopolitical news to cause a stir with the ceremonies in Jerusalem of the U.S. embassy move and the anniversary of the formation of Israel seventy years ago today. A number of Palestinian deaths occurred with many injuries as a result of strong protests and attempts to quell the excitement of the day.

5/15/18

It was a downer day Dude. The indices closed off of the lows of the day though and that was helpful. The S&P opened down at 2719 (-11) and reached an intraday low of 2702 (-28) prior to recovering to close at 2711, down 19. The Dow opened down at 24810, down 89 and reached an intraday low of 24629 (-270) before closing at 24706, down 193. The Nas opened at 7361, down 50 and reached an intraday low of 7321 (-90) before recovering to close at 7352, down 60. Today's action was not a surprise because the indices have been positive of late. The fly in the ointment was the VIX that closed up at 14.63. It closed above its 200 Day SMA. Not a thrilling move but one that needs continued observation. I did consider shifting more into our S&P fund but am waiting for more positive signs that a recession is not on the horizon.

5/16/18

Not much to say about the markets today. Seems as if we are slowly returning to normal meaning no wild gyrations intraday. The S&P opened at 2713 and reached an intraday high of 2728 before closing at

2722, up 11. The Dow opened at 24722 and reached 24801 (+95) before closing at 24769, up 63. The Nas opened at 7356 and reached 7413 intraday before closing at 7398, up 47. The VIX closed down below its 200 Day SMA to 13.42. That was certainly welcoming. The 10-year yield ended at 3.095. The last time it was at this level was in 2011. The only threats are a rising ten-year yield and some geopolitical events ongoing in the middle east that doesn't seem to be affecting the markets.

5/17/18

Like yesterday, the markets were consolidating. Excitement levels continue to modify and indices intraday trade fairly closely. The S&P opened at 2720 and ranged between 2711 (-11) and 2732 (+10) before closing at 2720, down 2 points. The Dow opened at 24752 and reached an intraday high of 24839 (+70) and a low of 24639 (-130) before closing at 24723, up 9 on the day. The Nas opened at 7380 and reached a high of 7425 (+27) and a low of 7350 (-48), closing at 7382, down 16. The VIX rose slightly to 13.46.

5/18/18

Another sideways day. This week's close is the second in a row that the Dow and S&P lost ground, although not by much. There is no excitement and that's not necessarily a bad thing. Have to admit that I miss the daily increases experienced through most of January.

The S&P opened at 2717 before reaching a low of 2709 (-11). The index closed at 2713, down 7. The Dow opened at down slightly at 24708. It reached an intraday high of 24775 (+61) and a low of 24665 (-49) before closing at 24715, up 1. The Nas opened at 7364, down 18, and reached a low of 7344 (-38) before closing at 7354, down 28. Not bad given the run up MTD. The VIX remains well behaved closing down slightly to 13.42.

The T/A and P&F sums have been over 1 for the last 10 of 11 days. Both categories have been participating and this trending is bullish. As of today, I am 2/3 invested in S&P and Fidelity International.

5/21/18

New week and renewed optimism with today's trading. The S&P opened up at 2726 and reached an intraday high of 2739 before closing at 2733, up 20. It would have been better to see a close above 2742 or thereabouts because it would have been the highest close since mid-March. We have a whole week though to make it happen. The Dow opened 168 points higher and was up to 25086 (+371) intraday before closing at 25013, up 298 points. It did close above a mid-March high of 25000. The Nas opened at 7406, up 52 and reached an intraday high of 7432 (+78) before losing steam to close at 7394, up 40. I still have a concern that a right shoulder might be forming and am keeping a wary eye out. The VIX closed at 13.10, down 2.4%.

Many are still skeptical that we have concluded the correction, but I still see cash inflows in both the Nasdaq and NYSE. So, I am growing cautiously optimistic with each new trading day.

5/22/18

The good news was that my T/A and P&F sums are slowly getting more positive, the VIX was relatively unchanged and cash was positive again on the NYSE and Nasdaq. Oil is still rising as forecasted and WTI reached 72.90. The 10 year though is at 3.065. But the Dow gave up most of yesterday's gain.

The S&P opened at 2738, up 5 and reached 2742 intraday (+9) and a low of 2722 (-11) before closing at 2724, down 9. The Dow opened at 25048, up 35 before reaching 25065 (+52) intraday and an intraday low of 24812 (-201). It closed at 24834 down 179. The Nas was positive most of the day after opening at 7421, up 27. It reached an intraday high of 7433 (+39) and a low of 7370 (-24) before closing at 7378, down 16.

5/23/18

The indices opened down but recovered by the COB. The VIX raised eyebrows too during most of the session but ended by closing down at 12.56, down 5% after reaching 14.60. The 10-year closed just slightly above 3.00.

The S&P opened at 2714, down 10 and reached an intraday low of 2710 (-14) before closing at 2733, up 9 points. The Dow opened at 24758, down 76 and reached an intraday low of 24667, down 167. Things started improving at around the announcement that the FED was willing to allow the inflation rate to remain above 2%, as long as it was behaving benignly. The index closed at 24887, up 52. The Nas opened at 7335, down 43 and the intraday low. It closed at 7426, up 47. I'm still waiting to see it move well above 7525 to begin negating a right shoulder formation. I'll keep an eye out but am not worried now. One can't negate the continued geopolitics going on with Iran, China trade and N. Korea's next statements about a June 12 conference on nuke disposal as a condition of any favorable regard on the part of the U.S.

5/24/18

See Saw day again. Because of recent negative communications from N. Korea, Trump announced that he has cancelled the June 12 summit. Markets reaction was of course negative, so the bulls aren't fully in charge.

The S&P opened at 2731, down 2. It reached an intraday low of 2707 (-26) but eventually moved back up to close at 2728, down 6, after reaching an intraday high of 2732. The Dow opened at 24877, down 10 and reached an intraday low of 24606, down 281. It recovered to its opening value before closing at 24812, down 75. The Nas opened at 7422, down 4. It reached an intraday low of 7358 (-68) and later reached its intraday high of 7435 (+9) before closing down slightly at 7424, down 2. The T/A and P&F sums continue to show improvement, so I am resting easy.

5/25/18

Summer for all intents and purposes begins this Memorial Day weekend. For traders it started today. You can usually explain away low volume when coming up on a three-day weekend. And the indices saw a lackluster day as a result.

The S&P opened at 2724 (-4) and reached an intraday low of 2715 (-13) before recovering somewhat to close at 2721, down 6. The Dow opened down at 24781 (-31) and reached an intraday low of 24688 (-124) before recovering somewhat to close at 24753, down 59. The Nas opened at 7422 (-2) and reached an intraday high of 7453 (+29) and a low of 7416 (-8) before closing at 7434, up 9.

The VIX closed up at 13.22 but still below its rising 200 Day SMA, a good sign regarding ant threat of increased volatility. Another important move today was the 10-year yield. It closed down at 2.93. Also positive was the T/A and P&F sums which moved back over 1. The bull 20 SMA P&F is nearing the bear P&F in value and will hopefully surpass it during next week. If it does it will be the first time since February 14. The longer I continue this spreadsheet the more comfortable I am that it is a great forecasting tool. The P&F summations are probably the most important, but the spreadsheet is easy to maintain with summing both the T/A and P&F columns.

5/29/18

Just when you began to believe that all things pointed to a market getting back on track a day like today comes along that provides a dose of fear. The Dow and S&P both suffered 1%+ losses. The prevailing belief had to do with a fear that Italy's formation of a new government that would attempt to quit the Euro. This news caused selling of bank stocks and caused treasury yields to fall. The VIX made a fairly significant move as well closing at 17 after rising to 18.8 intraday. The drops in the S&P and Dow were also steep for two other reasons in my belief. There was selling I'm sure, by those who follow the "sell in May" adage and a short trading week.

The S&P opened at 2705 (-16) and hit an intraday low of 2677 (-44) before recovering some of the losses to close at 2690, down 31. The Dow opened at 24607 (-146) and reached 24248 (-505) intraday. It recovered some of the loss in the late afternoon to close at 24361, down 392. The Nas fared much better opening at 7399 (-34) and reached an intraday low of 7354 (-80) before closing at 7397, down 37.

The T/A and P&F sums ended below 1.

I have to admit that confidence in decision making was important today. As the indices continued down throughout the day, I did not experience the anxieties that I have in the past. I kept an eye on the charts and the VIX. Hopefully, this is just a one- or two-day affair and the selling will simply expedite a return to more stability going forward.

5/30/18

Finally, the bull P&F 20 SMA has exceeded the bear 20 SMA for the first time since Feb. 14! And today was a recovery day from yesterday's losses. It's telling that the Dow and S&P both remained above their 50 EMA given that things could have gone either way following yesterday's losses. The VIX closed lower at 14.97 and the 10-year treasury yield recovered to 2.842 as well.

The S&P opened higher at 2702 (+12) and reached an intraday high of 2729 (+39) before dropping a bit to close at 2724, up 34. The Dow opened higher as well at 24468 (+107) and reached an intraday high of 24714 (+353) before closing at 24668, up 306. The Nas opened up as well at 7428 (+31) and reached 7473 (+76) before closing at 7462, up 66. Hopefully, the indices are ready to go into rally mode for a few weeks now.

5/31/18

Tariff talk was today's Debbie Downer, as Canada announced its own measures against U.S. products. You could watch the indices fall while Trudeau and the EU both denounced the U.S. tariffs and imposed their own in retaliation. It's good for our U.S. companies though. So be it.

The S&P opened at 2721 and hit an intraday low of 2701 (-23) before closing at 2705, down 19. The good news is that it closed the month with a 57 point gain. That's the highest month end close since Feb. 28. The Dow opened at 24621 (-47) and hit an intraday low of 24352 (-316) before gaining some ground to close at 24416, down 252. This month end close is the best since Feb. 28 as well. The Nas opened down as well at 7456 and reached 7431 (-31) before recovering somewhat to close at 7442, down 20. The VIX as you might imagine gained somewhat and closed at 15.43. It was as high as 16.29.

6/01/18

Not a bad week all in all. Turned out to be a big "W" actually. That is typically bullish. Time will tell. To recap: Tuesday was a Debbie Downer, Wednesday was a recovery day, Thursday, another Debbie Downer and today – an up day.

The S&P opened up at 2719 (+14) and reached 2737 intraday (+32) before closing at 2735, up 29. The Dow likewise opened up at 24542 (+126) and achieved an intraday high of 24674 (+258) before closing at 24635, up 219. Of course, it would have been great to see these indices close at the highs for the day but, that has been a rare occurrence over the last four months. The Nas remains on a tear opening at 7488 (+46) and reached an intraday high of 7557 before closing at 7554, up 112. The Nas was up 120 points for the week, the Dow was down 118 points and the Nas ended the week up 14.

The VIX ended at 13.46 and the 10 year closed the week at 2.895, far short of 3, which is the new magic

number.

6/04/18

I don't care for negative surprises and there was one today involving the P&F sums. When the indices continue improving, I have expectations of positive T/A s and P&F sums. The P&F ratio turned negative today for the first time since May 7. Cash for the NYSE has been negative as well. There are also concerns with the Dow and S&P narrow trading ranges. On the immediate surface I have been viewing things positively until today's P&F change. If the Dow doesn't get past 25000 and/or the S&P close above 2748 it may be time to close out of at least the S&P fund. So, I am now more cautious than I have been recently.

The S&P opened at 2742 (+7) and reached an intraday high of 2749 (+14) before closing at 2747, up 12. The Dow opened at 24728 (+93) and reached 24859 (+224) intraday before closing at 24814, up 178. The Nas opened at 7570 (+16) and reached 7607 (+53) intraday before closing at 7606, up 52. It is now just 31 points from its previous 52 week high in March. It has certainly been outperforming the other indices and logic would dictate, leading the way for the others. Time will tell of course.

6/05/18

The S&P managed 2753 intraday early on but resistance was too much as it closed at 2749, up 2. It was as low as 2740 (-7) before rising into the close. This will be an interesting test because if it doesn't move past the 2750-52 area it will likely mean a retest of a rising 50 Day SMA.

More precarious is the Dow. It needs to shoot above 25150 soon or a test of its 50 Day SMA is certain. The 200 Day SMA is rising quickly. Hopefully, these two averages will stay at a safe distance from each other.

The Dow did open slightly up at 24820 and rose to 24839 (+25) before hitting an intraday low of 24711 (-103). It did proceed higher through the rest of the afternoon to close at 24800, down 14.

The Nas opened at 7621 (+15) and hit 7644 (+38) before losing ground to close at 7638, up 31. The intraday high and close exceeded the previous intraday high of 7637 that was set in March.

The VIX closed at 12.48 and remained below its 200 Day SMA throughout the day. The T/A and P&F sums remained over 1. The P&F sums are negative for the second day running which is of concern to me. It is difficult to bet which way the markets go tomorrow and safe to say that I won't be surprised regardless of direction.

6/6/18

Today is the anniversary of the D-Day invasion of June 6, 1944.

Today was a definite plus from a technical perspective because the S&P soundly pushed to a close of 2722, the highest close since Mar. 12. It broke through the resistance of 2748/50 that has been so frustrating these past few months and should have clear sailing at least until 2802. The index opened up at 2753 and saw choppiness early before moving to 2772 where it closed, up 24.

The Dow cleared the 25100, that had been the top of the resistance area previously. The last close above 25000 was Mar. 13. It opened at 24854 (+54) and continued higher throughout the day. It closed at its high of the day at 25146, up 346.

The Nas opened up 15 at 7653 but then hit a little profit taking early reaching an intraday low of 7622 (-16) before joining the party to close at 7689, up 51. This was a new high and just short of its intraday high of 7692.

My T/A and P&F sums concerns were put to rest with a positive P&F ratio. The VIX dropped 6% to end at 11.66. That of course is very positive as well. The last time it closed that low was Jan. 25. The NYSE and Nasdaq both reflected cash positive by the last hour or so of the trading day.

6/7/18

Just a ho-hum day and due after 4days of advances for the S&P. the Dow was the only major to close up. The S&P opened up 3 and eventually moved to an intraday high of 2780 (+8) before changing direction to hit an intraday low of 2760 (-12). It perked up during the last two hours to close at 2770, down2. This kind of activity is to be expected while the index tries to get traction to eventually close above 2802 or so, just 30 points away after today but a move that could take some time.

The Dow opened at 25192 (+46) and reached a peak of 25326 (+180) before closing at 25241, up 95. The Nas opened at 7697 (+8) and that was its high for the day. There was obvious profit taking going on after the great run it had since the middle of May. The index hit 7598 (-91) intraday but gained enough ground to close at 7635, down 54.

The VIX rose to 12.07 but remains well below its 200 Day SMA. All other related activities are very positive as well.

6/8/18

The week finished with the major indices on the plus side. The S&P opened down 2766 (-4) and reached an intraday low of 2764 before recovering to close up at 2779, up 9. It was up 44 points for the week. The Dow opened at 25209 (-32) and hit an intraday low of 25166 (-75) but recovered to close at 25317, up 75 points. The Dow gained 682 points for the week. The Nas opened down at 7608 (-27) and dropped to an intraday low of 7595 (-40) before recovering to close at 7646, up 10. The Nas gained 92 for the week.

The VIX rose to 13.31 in early trading but closed at 12.17, up .04. Even at its high it was well below its 200 Day SMA. The T/A and P&F sums remain very positive. No complaints about the week.

It is time to look at the RSIs for each index though because these could be reaching overbought conditions sometime next week. Some pullbacks would be welcome. The RSI for the daily Nas is 68.17. The daily S&P is at 64.65, and the Dow is at 63.57. In a rising market RSIs can remain overbought for some time before seeing a pullback or correction. Modest daily increases of .3% or so would be ideal now but it usually doesn't happen like that. Time will tell.

6/11/18

The historic meeting between Un and Trump will take place in four and one-half hours (@9 pm) and you could see some panic selling in the last hour. All of the indices were doing well from the get-go and all were much higher intraday.

The VIX rose somewhat to close at 12.40. It remains well below its 200 Day SMA. Incoming cash was very positive with the NASDAQ and so-so with the NYSE. The T/A and P&F sums were positive as well. All things considered, a good day.

The S&P opened at 2780 (+1) and hit an intraday high of 2790 (+11) before closing at 2782, up 3. This will likely be the scenario for a week or three because of resistance immediately below 2802.

The Dow opened at 25337 (+20) and reached an intraday high of 25403 (+86) before closing at 25322, up 6.

The Nas opened at 7647 (+1) and reached an intraday high of 7677 (+31) before closing at 7660, up 14.

All-in-all a good day. These kinds of days keep the RSIs reasonable and PPOs and PMOs positive. The day's highs were actually reflecting too much exuberance in my opinion and the lower closes tamped the flame.

6/12/18

Another good day for the markets. There were no extremes as a result of the Trump/Un meeting, something that could have resulted in either a buying or selling frenzy.

The S&P opened at 2786 (+4) and advanced to an intraday high of 2790 (+8) before closing at 2787, up 5. The Dow opened at 25347 (+25) and reached an intraday high of 25364 (+42) and an intraday low of 25247 (-75) before attempting a positive close to no avail. The index closed at 25321, down not quite 2. The Nas resumed its forward progress with an opening of 7674, up 14. It hit an intraday day high of 7708 (+48) before closing at 7704, up 44. 7708 was a new high.

The VIX closed at 12.30 and the 10-year closed at 2.957.

The markets are not overheating given that the daily RSIs remain below 70.

6/13/18

I was watching CNBC when the Feds announced that they were raising the rate a quarter of a percent to 2.00. No surprise there because unless you were living under a rock you knew this was coming. What some didn't anticipate was that there would likely be two more increases this year. But even that should not have been a surprise because this has also been discussed often. So, the markets went into a tizzy at 2:00 pm and sold off the rest of the day. That is really a good thing though because it keeps the markets from overheating. So, the stats of the day.

The S&P opened at 2788, up 1 and reached an intraday high of 2791 (+4) and a low of 2775 (-12) before closing at 2776, down 11. The Dow opened at 25329 (+8) and reached an intraday high of 25362 (+41) and a low of 25191 (-130) before closing at 25201, down 120. The Nas opened at 7714 (+10) and hit a new high of 7749 (+45). It later tailed down somewhat to a low of 7687 (-17) before closing at 7696, down 8. The VIX was positive for a change closing up at 12.94. It remains well below its 200 Day SMA. The 10-year yield ended at 2.977 and that should not have been a surprise given the FED rate increase.

6/14/18

The Nas is really burning rubber and the S&P and Dow watched the smoke. The Dow was down slightly after being up in the early morning while the S&P gained back about half of yesterday's loss. Of the three it is the Nas that concerns me because remains overbought with an RSI of 73.58. It needs a cooling off period but that's just my concern.

The S&P opened up at 2783 (+7) and reached an intraday high of 2789 before retreating to close at 2782, up 7. (rounding).

The Dow opened up at 25255 (+54) and hit 25332 (+131) before changing direction to close at 25175, down 26. Both indices are fighting their mid-March resistance. My expectation is this kind of sideways movement until supply dries up at those levels of resistance.

The booming Nas hit another new high intraday of 7769 before closing at 7761, up 65. It opened at 7724 (+28) its low of the day.

Still, all-in-all, a pretty unremarkable day even considering the Nasdaq performance. The VIX ended down at 12.10 and the 10 year at 2.946. I expect more softening of this yield because its chart has

formed a short-term H&S. You might find it testing the lows of April and May somewhere at the 2.75 area.

6/15/18

It was a rush to judgement day for CNBC. The had on "experts" explaining that trade wars were imminent, the administration didn't know what it was doing, and that the WTO was going to put an end to U.S. tariffs. Right. Where was the WTO when the U.S. complained over the years about the Chinese unfair trade practices?

Basically, the major indices have been heating up fairly quickly, the Nas in particular, so this was just an oversupply day being administered to. And despite some early losses the indices ended the day and week in unremarkable closes. As a matter of fact, it was Chinese and European stocks that took the real drubbing.

The S&P opened at 2778 (-4) and reached an intraday low of 2762 (-20) before closing at 2779, down 3.

The Dow opened down at 25117 (-58) and reached 24894 (-281) intraday. It ended down at 25090, down 85. The Dow bounced off support established at its mid-April monthly high.

The Nas showed remarkable endurance today as it basically ignores any challenges to its leadership of late. It opened at 7725 (-36) and achieved a low of 7704 (-57) at which point buying took hold, ending at 7746, down 15). The index hit new highs during the week and closed up 100 points.

The VIX closed at 11.97 after reaching an early morning high of 13.16. The 10-year closed down again at 2.924 and below its 50 Day SMA.

All-in-all, it was a pretty good week for the overall market and the Nas in particular.

6/18/18

Traders were skittish today. The headliners are blaming trade and tariffs, but I believe it also has a lot to do with immigration issues in the U.S. but more importantly in Germany. There is talk that Merkel could be on her way out because of her staunch defense of permissive immigration. This has been an ongoing issue so time will tell.

The indices were promising very negative openings since last night and materialized at the opening bell. The S&P opened at 2766 (-14) and achieve3d an intraday low of 2757, down 23, after the opening bell. It remained in the red all day but recovered to close at 2774, down 6.

The Dow opened at 24944, down 146 and hit a low of 24826, down 264. Like the S&P it spent the rest of the day recovering lost ground to close at 24987, down 103. Hat to see it close below 25000 bit it is what it is. Names like Boeing and Caterpillar led the way down because of the dependency on international sales.

The Nas opened at 7693, down 53, before reaching 7677, down 69 intraday. Unlike its brethren the Nas managed to eke out a small gain of 1, closing at 7747.

The VIX hit an intraday high of 13.74, (the 200 Day SMA was 13.85) before retreating to 12.31 at the close. The 10-year closed at 2.93. The T/A and P&F sums equaled exactly 1.0. That's the first time that's happened. Nothing significant, just interesting. Maybe we'll have the winning numbers on Wednesday's Megabucks draw.

6/19/18

Another day with traders enthralled with tariffs. Nothing to report regarding Merkel. All indices opened down and remained that way until the close.

The S&P opened at 2752 (-22) and reached an intraday low of 2743, down 31. It pulled out of its dive throughout the day and closed at 2763, down 11. The Dow fared worse and closed at a loss for the year. It opened at 24764 (-223) and reached an intraday low of 24568, down 419. It struggled throughout the day to close at 24700, down 287. Like yesterday, Boeing and Caterpillar led the way. The Nas opened at 7658 (-89) reaching an intraday low of 7636, down 111, before recovering most of its loss to close at 7726, down 21.

The VIX did close up at 13.35. It blew thru its 200 Day SMA, but only briefly and closed below it, a positive sign. I also noticed that cash was positive for the NYSE but negative for the Nasdaq. My T/A and P&F sums were below 1. But that's three days now at or below 1.0. I also review the "WSJ Market Data Center Money Flows". It tracks money flow and significant block trades. I am looking for unusual selling and haven't noticed anything that concerns me.

In my opinion there has been a good deal of negative news as regards tariff issues and immigration both here and abroad. It sways traders, regardless of what you read. As bad as the sell-off seemed it was worse for China and Europe. I believe that issues between China and the U.S. will resolve before Saturday, in part because of the beatings on the Asian exchanges and because China realizes it has had it too good for too long.

6/20/18

Markets were up across the globe today including the major U.S. indices with the exception of the Dow. Newsworthy was the executive order that ended the practice of separating families at the detention centers. There has been an ongoing roar of disapproval since last week.

The S&P opened higher at 2770 (+7) and reached an intraday high of 2775 (+12) before losing steam to close at 2767, up 5.

The Dow opened up as well at 24771 (+71) and reached an intraday high of 24805 (+105) and a low of 24628 (-72). It closed down at 24658, down 42. Like yesterday the Dow penetrated its rising 50 Day SMA but managed to close slightly above it. I am in hopes that it remains support.

The Nas hit a new high today of 7807. It opened at 7764 (+38) and went briefly to 7807 (+81) before closing at 7782, up 56. It is slightly overbought with an RSI of 72. It would be good to see the gap up created today to get filled in sooner than later.

The VIX closed at 12.79 and the 10 year at 2.93. The T/A and P&F sums were over 1.

The tariff issues are still unsettled so I'm not expecting anything dramatic in terms of breakouts for the S&P and Dow. The resistance is clearly there for both indices, so it will take some good news and time to chew up the supply.

6/21/18

Summer came today but there was no warmth in the trading day unless you were short. The indices were down overnight and never recovered.

The S&P opened at 2769 (+2) and scurried to a low of 2744 (-23) at around 3:30. It retraced somewhat to close at 2750, down 18 on the day.

The Dow had been closing above its 50 Day SMA until today. With that line of defense gone the 200 Day SMA is within 200 points of today's close. Hopefully it will hold.

The Dow opened at 24639 just slightly down but reached an intraday low of 24407 (-251) at about the same time as the low was hit for the S&P. It closed at 24462, down 196.

The Nas got a little bloodied as well today. It opened at 7800 (+18) and managed an intraday high of 7803 before reaching a low of 7699 (-83) before closing at 7713, down 69. This was actually good because it brought the RSI some breathing room and also closed yesterday's gap. It too hit its low at 3:30. With all three indices turning at 3:30 it might mean capitulation, at least for the time being.

My sums closed at less than 1, the VIX closed up at 14.64 and above its 50 and 200 Day SMA. That concerns me because it broke out of a descending pennant pattern as well.

6/22/18

Comments from a couple of StockCharts.com principals have concerned me as well. For several days now, the trend has been selling late into the day. Today was no different. All indices opened higher and basically traded up until near the close at which point selling took over. At any rate I feel more at ease than I have been this past few days. I will also add that the bullish T/A and P&F adds have been on a decreasing trend and the bearish increasing over the last week. The day closed over 1 but this trend is down as well. I do have to be able to sleep at night after all, so I am at ease with moving more to near cash and leaving less than half still invested.

The S&P opened at 2761 (+11) and reached an intraday high of 2764 (+14) before turning tail in the late afternoon to close at 2755, up 5.

The Dow opened at 24527 (+65) and reached an intraday high of 24663 (+201) but like the S&P changed course to close at 24581, up 119). This was the first time in nine days that the Dow closed positive.

The Nas is the only index that has been consistently positive although it closed lower. It opened at 7740 (+27) and didn't go any higher. It reached an intraday low of 7679 (-34) before closing at 7693, down 20.

The VIX closed down at 13.75, below both its 50 and 200 Day SMA. Just barely as concerns the 200 Day SMA that is at 13.90. The 50 and 200 Day SMA are just a few days away from a crossover, but I now have my doubts because of this week's behavior chart wise. The Dow managed to rise to its 50 Day SMA but retreated. This is not a good outcome and means support is at its 200 Day SMA which is only 313 points below today's close. In addition, the PMOs and PPOs of the major indices have crossed their respective signal lines. Time will tell, but at this juncture there are too many negative signals for me to be heavily invested especially over the weekend.

6/25/18

If you like occasional market mayhem, then today was one of those days! You could sense something was brewing with the way the markets dropped so quickly during the last 30 minutes of the trading day. The futures were heading south last night and were even worse by the opening bells. The VIX was already over 15 by then as well. From 9:30 on it was a grand rush south on all leading indices.

The S&P opened at 2743 (-12) and reached an intraday low of 2699 (-56) before closing at 2717, down 38.

The Dow opened at 24464 (-117) and reached an intraday low of 24084 (-497) before closing at 24253, down 328.

The Nas opened at 7631 (-62) and fell to 7478 (-215) before recovering to 7532, down 161.

The S&P broke through its 50 Day SMA but managed to close slightly above it by less than a point. There might be a bounce tomorrow, but I expect it to follow suit with the Dow and close below it. The Dow closed below its 200 Day SMA and may well drop to 23500 (early May low) before ending its consolidation, hopefully for good. The Nas closed well above its 50 Day SMA, although it could make a run for it as early as tomorrow.

The VIX opened at 15.07 (+1.32) and reached a high of 19.61 before closing at 17.48. It closed well above its 50 and 200 Day SMAs. That's not good and hopefully short lived. The T/A and P&F sums were .41, well below 1.

Traders and investors are worried about trade issues for sure. But these will end favorably. I think a bigger issue is the border, though it goes unsaid. From my perspective there is nothing new here that hasn't been going on for years. I do believe that it contributes to that single issue that can cause the most trading grief though coupled with the trade issues – uncertainty.

6/26/18

All indices closed in the green. But if you were reading more than headlines, you'd note that the patterns established about two weeks ago haven't changed. The markets generally have been opening higher with few exceptions, hit intraday highs and then sold off much of the day's gain in the last hour or so. A better pattern is seeing gains hold to the close and that hasn't been happening.

The S&P opened at 2722 (+5) and reached an intraday high of 2733 (+16) before losing wind to close at 2723, up 6. It closed above its 50 Day SMA that was 2717 today and rising. I believe it will close below that at some point this week.

The Dow also opened up at 24282 (+29) and reached an intraday high of 24384 (+131) before losing altitude to close at 24283, up 30. It closed below both SMAs as it did yesterday.

The Nas opened up at 7554 (+22) and reached an intraday high of 7597 (+65) before its retreat to close at 7562, up 30. It remains above its 50 and 200 Day SMAs for the time being.

The T/A and P&F sums remain below 1. The P&F positive was lower than yesterday and the negative higher. The VIX closed at 15.96 and remains well above its 50 and 200 Day SMAs. Today's candle had a real body that was inside yesterday's candle so I'm guessing that it will continue down for the time being. TIC (crude) closed above 70 for the first time this month. I still expect it to hit 80 at some point soon. The 10-year yield is at 2.88. I'm still looking for it to fall further as mentioned earlier.

6/27/18

Schizophrenic kind of day to say the least. The pre-market was negative with a triple digit drop for the Dow that suddenly shifted to green around 8:00 am. All indices were up nicely until noon. Then it was a service elevator ride down for the rest of the day. There are no technical reasons for being optimistic in the near term at least.

The S&P opened at 2728 (+5) and reached a high of 2746 (+23) before beginning its decline to close at 2700, down 23.

The Dow pretty much followed suit opening at 24303 (+20) and rose to 24569 (+286) before closing at 24118, down 166.

The Nas also opened up at 7586 (+24) and reached 7611 (+49) intraday, closing at 7445, down 117.

The S&P closed below its 50 Day SMA but stopped short of a trendline drawn from the first week in April as the start of an uptrend. It closed 33 points above its 200 Day SMA established today. The Nas remained 22 points above today's 50 Day SMA. The VIX closed at 17.91. It is running into an area of resistance but looks too have enough steam to go higher.

I'm looking forward to Friday's results because it will be the end of the week, month and quarter. As for trading tomorrow and Friday I have no expectations. The tea leaves are way to cloudy!

6/28/18

The longer that I maintain the T/A and P&F sums the more respect I have for it. Today's results were

very interesting or perhaps it doesn't happen often. The indices for the most part all closed higher and yet the T/A and F&F sums were lower in total. The P&F in particular results were lower than yesterdays. This is unusual after such a big difference from one day to the next. I have to conclude that we are in another (or just continuing) correction. It is like the line between love and hate. It is very thin. This is how the chart is behaving because of the ease of going positive to negative. That's what the last two weeks have been demonstrating at any rate. Another issue is that cash was positive for the Nas but negative for the NYSE. This isn't new which is pointing to further drops in the major indices. Enough on that.

The S&P opened at 2699, basically unchanged. It reached an intraday low of 2692 (-8) and a high of 2724 (+24) before closing at 2716, up 17.

The Dow opened at 24064 (-54) and hit an intraday low of 23997 (-121) and later a high of 24308 before losing air to close at 24216, up 98 points.

The Nas opened at 7438 (-7) and reached an intraday low of 7420 (-25) and a high of 7526 (+81) before closing at 7504, up 59.

So, the trend of moving in one direction all day and losing steam at day's end continues and this doesn't exude confidence. The VIX closed at 17.02. It failed to make a new high but is safely above its SMAs. The Nas bounced off its 50 Day SMA which was promising. The Dow hit its 200 Day SMA but retreated and the S&P closed ever so slightly below its 50 Day SMA. It did penetrate the moving average but retreated.

Perhaps tomorrow will reveal some hints about the market's general direction with the completion of quarter end reallocations.

6/29/18

It looked like rally mode beginning with the pre-market and lasting until about 3:00. Then the indices moved into the routine that has been practiced for about the last three weeks. Selling at the end of the day. I was even considering looking at a logical fund to put money into for about five seconds…and instead took more out at around noon. Of course, it doesn't happen until COB but I'm very unimpressed with the markets now and still leaning in the preservation of capital direction.

The S&P opened at 2727 (+11) and reached an intraday high of 2743 (+27) before closing at the low of the day at 2718, up 2.

The Dow opened at 24324 (+108) and cruised to 24510 (+294) and closed near its low of the day at 24271, up 55.

The Nas opened up as well at 7544 (+40) reaching 7574 (+70) before it too hightailed back to close at 7510, up 7.

My T/A and P&F improved but remains below 1. The VIX closed down somewhat at 15.97. Cash started positive for the Nas and NYSE but finished negative. Today was the end of the week, month and quarter as well as the first half of the year. The Nas started the year at 6903 and is up 607 points (8.8%). The S&P began the year at 2674 and is up 44 points (1.65%). The Dow ended 2017 at 24719 and is down 448 points (-1.8%). Hopefully we will see better results in the last half of the year. But it is mid-term for elections, so it will likely be a nail-biter going forward unless key races flesh out early. In other words, don't count on seeing any change at least until November 7!

July

7/02/18

The Dow was down triple digits pre-market and opened at 24161 (-110) and reached an intraday low of 24078 (-193). It started some recovery effort at about 1:30 and eventually closed at 24307, up 36. There have been three positive days in roughly three weeks for this index.

The S&P opened at 2705 (-13) and hit a low of 2699 intraday (-19) before doing a little rally by COB to close at 2727, up 8.

The Nas opened down at 7452 (-58) reaching an intraday low of 7443 (-67) before changing direction to close at 7568, up 57.

The Nas bounced strongly off its 50 Day SMA before recovering. Perhaps that's a good omen. I'm sure we will know better at tomorrow's close but that was technically a good signal. The S&P remained below its 50 Day SMA for a good part of the day but likewise closed above it for the first time since last Wednesday.

The VIX closed at 15.61, down from Friday's close but still above its SMAs. The T/A and P&F sums remain below 1 with continued deterioration.

7/03/18

Today was a short session with the NYSE and NASDAQ closing at 1:00. This is common on the day before a major holiday. Yesterday's session didn't get a replay today in fact it was the opposite with the indices opening up only to close down pretty significantly. It is worthwhile remembering that weeks with a midweek holiday usually incur lighter trading volumes.

The S&P opened up at 2733 (+6) and reached an intraday high of 2737 (+10) before dropping to 2711 (-16) intraday before closing at 2713, down 13.

The Dow opened at 24359 (+52) and reached an intraday high of 24445 (+138) and an intraday low of 24151 (-156), before closing at 24175, down 132.

The Nas also opened up at 7594 (+26) its high for the day. It reached an intraday low of 7498 (-70) before closing at 7503, down 65.

The all-important VIX closed higher at 16.14 after reaching a high of 16.45. My T/A and P&F sums did break back above 1 but not dramatically so. The S&P closed below its 50 Day SMA again while there were no changes to the Dow and Nas although the Dow did penetrate its 200 Day SMA briefly.

7/05/18

The market looked strong beginning with the pre-market. But of course, that hasn't been anything new of late. What was surprising was how well the market performed right up to the close.

The S&P opened at 2724 (+11) and never looked back reaching an intraday high of 2738 (+25) and closed at 2737, up 23. It closed above its 50 Day SMA. Let's hope it stays there.

The Dow opened at 24286 (+111) and reached an intraday high of 24373 (+198) before closing at 24357, up 182. It closed slightly above its 200 Day SMA.

The Nas opened at 7551 (+48) and reached an intraday high of 7589 (+86) before closing at 7586, up 84.

The VIX closed at 14.97 and my T/A and P&F sums were over 1. The bear P&F sum is still well above the bull total although it did improve. But one day's market action does not constitute a direction change and there are no technicals that indicate a favorable change.

7/06/18

We had strong closes for the second day in a row and very importantly, on a Friday. It helps break the trend that we have been seeing for a month.

The S&P opened at 2738 (+1) and reached an intraday low early of 2734 (-3) and an intraday high of 2764 (+27) and closed at 2760, up 23. It of course remains above its EMAs.

The Dow opened at 24352 (-5) and reached an intraday low of 24281 (-76). Although it took a while getting out of the gate it hit an intraday high of 24520 (+163) before losing some traction to close at 24456, up 100. This close was above its 200 EMA for the first time since last week, doing so with room to spare. Still, it has been a low volume week, so Monday will be a better predicter of where the Dow is headed.

The Nas opened at 7596 (+10) and reached 7696 (+110) before closing at 7688, up 102.

The T/A and P&F sums improved but the P&F side of the analysis is still negative. The VIX closed at 13.37 and that is a very nice indicator for an improving market climate. Cash was positive all day for the NASDAQ but static for the NYSE. This needs to change.

7/09/18

Third day in a row that the indices have closed at or near the daily highs. It is especially meaningful because traders should be back to work given that last week was a holiday one. This gives me more confidence, that and the fact that the major indices are all above their 50 EMA now.

The S&P opened at 2769 (+9) and reached 2785 (+25) intraday before closing at 2784, up 24.

The Dow opened at 24519 (+63) and climbed to 24797 (+341) before its close at 24777, up 320. That puts the Dow positive for the year by 58 points. Not great news but given the tumult of the first half it is certainly welcome.

The Nas opened at 7732 (+44) and reached an intraday high of 7757 (+69) to close at 7756, up 68. Another day like this will put the Nas at a new high.

All T/A aspects are positive. The all-important VIX closed down at 12.70 and below its SMAs. In fact, the 50 EMA closed below its 200 EMA. The last time the 200 EMA was above the 50 EMA was early February, the start of the correction.

7/10/18

And yet another nice close with a reasonably strong finish for the major indices and continued good signals from a technical analyses' perspective.

The S&P opened at 2789 (+5) and reached an intraday high of 2796 (+12) before losing some steam to close at 2794, up 10.

The Dow opened at 24807 (+30) and scrambled to 24945 (+168) before relaxing to close at 24920, up 143. This close placed a little more space between it and its recent closes above its SMAs. Its PMO is set to cross the signal line for the first time since mid-June.

The Nas opened at 7771 (+15) and did some retracing to an intraday low of (-24) after having hit a high of 7777 (+21). It closed up though at 7759 with a gain of 3. Obvious profit taking after such a nice recovery since June 27 when it closed at 7445.

I would expect to see some profit taking with the Dow and S&P as well over the course of the next few days, but it could be brief now that we are getting second quarter earnings reports.

The VIX closed lower again at 12.58 and my T/A and P&F sums are over 1 for the fifth consecutive day.

7/11/18

The market took a breather today after a bullish few days with blame being placed on tariff discussions.

The S&P opened at 2780 (-14) and hit an intraday low of 2771 (-23) before closing at 2774, down 20.

The Dow also opened lower at 24789 (-131) and reached 24664 (-256) intraday before closing at 24700, down 219.

The Nas opened at 7699 (-60) and dropped to a low intraday of 7697 (-62) before closing at 7717, down 43.

The VIX closed at 13.62 still below its moving averages. It did hit its 200 Day SMA, penetrating the 50 before dropping below both. The 50 Day SMA is below the 200 Day SMA now and that is a positive. My T/A and P&F sums are below 1.

7/12/18

You always like to see a close where the indexes are at their high/near high and today was one of those days. So, after yesterday's profit taking it would appear that resistance testing is getting serious.

The S&P opened at 2783 (+9) and reached 2799 (+25) late in the day and closed at 2798, up 24.

The Dow opened higher at 24803 (+103) reaching 24940 (+240) before closing at 24925, up 224.

The Nas opened up at 7753 (+36) and reached an intraday high of 7826 (+109) before closing at 7824, up 107. The intraday high was a record high for the index.

The VIX closed at 12.56 and never threatened its 50 Day SMA which is below its 200SMA. My T/A and P&F sums are back above 1 and the spread between the bullish/bearish P&F sums is widening. So, all-in-all it was a pretty good day. It will be good to see the Dow close above 25000 and the S&P close above 2800 tomorrow, as it appears strong enough in both cases to do so. From there the indices should challenge previous highs.

7/13/18

The S&P closed at 2801. The last time that it closed above 2800 was February 1st. It opened at 2797 (-1) and reached an intraday low of 2792 (-6) and an intraday high of 2805 (+7) and closed at 2801, up 3. The last time that the S&P was in the 2800 neighborhood was March 13. So, it was exciting to see it over 2800. It will likely move very little for the next few trading days but eventually shoot toward its previous high.

Not to be under the S&P shadow, the Dow closed above 25000. It opened at 24926 (+1) and reached an intraday low of 24890 (-35) and an intraday high of 25043 (+118). It closed at 25019, up 95. The Dow last closed above 25000 on June 15.

The Nas opened at 7828 (+4) and reached an intraday low of 7803 (-21) and a high of 7844 (+20). That was a new intraday high. The index closed at 7826, up 2.

My T/A and P&F sums were over 1 and a little lower than yesterday. Both the bullish and bearish P&F sums were higher. That doesn't happen often, but it will bear scrutiny. None of the RSIs reflect overbought conditions and the PMOs for the indices are higher than each of the signal lines. The VIX is at 12.18.

7/16/18

I finally transferred my balance from ICMA to a Fidelity IRA. I do need to be careful that my trading is induced by technical information and will likely stay with Fidelity ETFs and iShares. Now the day's results.

The S&P opened even reaching an intraday high of 2804 (+3) and a low of 2793 (-8) before closing at 2798, down 3.

The Dow opened at 25026 (+7) and reached a low of 24980 (-39) and an intraday high of 25072 (+53) before closing at 25064, up 45.

The Nas opened up at 7832 (+6) reaching an intraday high of 7839 (+16) and a low of 7792 (-34) before closing at 7806, down 20.

The VIX closed up at 12.83 but still below its SMAs. The 10 year is still in a sideways movement and WTIC closed below its 50 Day SMA for the first time in about three weeks.

7/17/18

Today I learned that Fidelity ETFs don't necessarily keep up with percentage changes of related ETFs. But I wouldn't have known unless I bought them. There was no commission for buying, just selling. Volumes just aren't the same either. I will stick with more actively traded ETFs, at least for the time being.

It was a good day for the market with major indices rising. After the Dow broke 25000 and the S&P 2800 it could be smooth sailing for a bit.

The S&P opened at 2789 (-9) and rose the remainder of the day with an intraday high of 2814 (+16) before closing at 2810, up 11.

The Dow opened at 25034 (-30) and reached an intraday low of 24990 (-74) and a high of 25155 (+91) before closing at 25120, up 56.

The Nas opened well below the previous close at 7752, off 54. It rose though through the day to hit a new intraday high of 7867 (+61) before closing at 7855, up 49.

The VIX made an effort to climb higher and reached 13.18. That was well below its SMAs, so no perceived angst today. It closed down 12.04. Mt T/A and P&F almost reached 1 today ending at .97. The 10 year is at 2.864.

7/18/18

Another good day for the markets. The best way to describe it is that it was pretty stable with little fanfare and intraday spreads between highs and lows.

The S&P opened at 2811 (+1) and hit a high of 2817 (+7) before closing at 2816, up 6.

The Dow opened at 25134 (+14) reaching an intraday low of 25101 (-19) and a high of 25215 (+95) before closing at 25199, up 79.

The Nas hit another intraday new high after opening at 7859 (+4) and proceeded south for some profit taking to 7823 (-32). It hit 7864 (+9) and closed at 7854, down 1.

This is a time to be cautious because second quarter earnings are being disclosed in ever greater corporations reporting. This is nothing like January's reporting when the markets were over-heated but still worth being cautious for any negative forecasts.

My T/A and P&F sums are over 1 again with P&F bullish values. The VIX closed up slightly but was never a concern today.

7/19/18

The majors took a breather today although closing above 2800 for the S&P and 25000 for the Dow. That and the fact that my T/A and P&F sums remained above 1. The VIX closed at 12.87. That remains below the SMAs.

The S&P opened at 2809 (-7) and hit an intraday low of 2800 (-16) and a high of 2812 (-4) before closing at 2804, down 11.

The Dow opened at 25139 (-60) and hit an intraday low of 25053 (-146) before closing down at 25064, down 135.

The Nas opened at 7830 (-24) and hit an intraday low of 7811 (-43) before closing at 7825, down 29.

The down day kept the indices from heading to overbought territory. The Nas has been hitting record highs and it is my belief that the Dow and S&P will soon be following based on the charts that I keep including the VIX. I am long on SPY, FNCL (financial ETF), FTEC (information technology ETF), USO and XOP. I especially like USO because oil has been trending higher and XOP because NG storage is at a near five year low and will go lower should the summer remain hot.

7/20/18

The early pre-market (0645) had all the makings of a bad trading day. As the morning progressed the pre-market improved with barely a hint of the earlier staging.

The S&P opened flat and had an intraday high of 2810 (+6) and a low of 2800 (-4) before closing at 2802, down 2 (rounding).

The Dow opened at 25041 (-23) and reached an intraday low of 24986 (-78) early in the session and a high of 25124 (+60) before closing at 25058, down 6.

The Nas opened at 7843 (+18), reaching an intraday high of 7860 (+35) and a low of 7816 (-9) before closing at 7820, down 5. Given all of the recent talking points of tariffs and the Trump/Putin summit, I'd say the markets did well. The Dow and S&P are definitely testing their respective new-found support.

The VIX closed at 12.86 after opening at 13.00 and reaching 13.58 intraday, its 50 Day SMA. I consider that as a positive. My T/A and P&F were above 1. The 10 year did rise to 2.895. We'll need to watch this.

7/23/18

The Dow closed lower but remained above 25000 while the Nas and S&P closed higher. Complacency in the markets seems the norm and I think it is cause for concern because we are in the thick of earnings season now and to date the reports have been excellent. Oil closed flat, and the 10 year rose to 2.965. The VIX closed down at 12.62.

The S&P opened down 3 at 2799 and fell to an intraday low of 2795 (-7) before changing direction to a reach a high of 2809 (+7) before closing at 2807, up 5.

The Dow opened at 25037 (-21) and reached an intraday low of 24983 (-75) and a high of 25081 (+23) before closing at 25044, down 14.

The Nas opened at 7843 (+23) but proceeded south for a while to hit a low of 7777 (-43). It changed course and hit a high of 7847 (+27) before closing at 7842, up 22.

I closed my XOP position because of the negative T/A. I expected improvement with a rise in oil prices which really hasn't changed much since last week. I did break even although that's not a goal.

7/24/18

Not a bad day but certainly an interesting one. The indices were all very positive pre-market and quickly moved up at the opening bell. In fact, the Nas hit a record high early on and then immediately headed south. The Dow and S&P started off nicely as well but lost track in the afternoon. These indices did recover lost ground especially in the last half hour of trading. To see that kind of confidence is always good, even if it's just for overnight.

The S&P opened at 2821 (+14) and reached a high intraday of 2830 (+23) before closing at 2820, up 13.

The Dow opened at 25092 (+48) and hit an intraday high of 25287 (+243) before closing at 25242, up 198.

The Nas opened at 7914 (+72) and proceeded to an intraday record high of 7929 (+87) and a low of 7814 (-28) before turning around to close at 7841, down 1. This activity does bear watching to ensure it wasn't a blow-off top.

The VIX moved higher to 13.21 early but closed down at 12.41. The 10-year closed down at 2.949 but the 2-year closed up at 2.64. This bears watching closely because banks borrow at that rate so the greater the spread between the two the better for lending.

7/25/18

What an outstanding final 20 +/- minutes the markets enjoyed today! This as a result of a meeting between the U.S. and EU concerning the easing of trade relations between us and the EU. During those roughly 20 minutes the Dow rose roughly 150 points, the S&P roughly 12 and the Nas roughly 39 points!

The markets have been skittish over the tariff results for several weeks now, so any promise of a resolution would favorably affect that behavior and you saw the results at the close. This was also the first time in a few months that I saw cash moving in unison to the NYSE and NASDAQ, also a favorable sign.

The S&P opened 2818 (-2) and improved throughout the day albeit without much enthusiasm. It reached an intraday high of 2848 (+28) before closing at 2846, up 26. The S&P is now within 27 points of its all-time high of 2873.

The Dow opened down at 25184 (-58) and reached an intraday low of 25114 (-128) before moving higher to reach an intraday high of 25433 (+191) before closing at 25414, up 172.

The Nas opened at 7839 (-2) and reached an intraday high of 7933 (+92) before closing off that high at 7932 for a new closing high, up 91. The Nas has been the Energizer Bunny lately and I would like to see the S&P follow suit.

The VIX closed down at 12.20. The 10 and 2 year treasuries closed down as well.

7/26/48

Zuckerberg took a drubbing today losing around $16 billion in value to his FB holdings. That also opened the door to skepticism on many tech stocks causing the Nas and S&P to lose ground. The Dow on the other hand did well, probably because of yesterday's media event with the president and EU chair.

The S&P opened at 2835 (-11). That was the intraday low. It improved somewhat to close at 2837, down 9. It is now 36 points from its all-time high.

The Dow opened at 25469 (+55) and achieved a high of 25587 (+173) before closing at 25527, up 113. It is 1090 points away from its all-time high and closing.

The Nas took the bullet today thanks to FB and related SM stocks. It opened down at 7848 (-84) and hit an intraday low of 7834 (-98) before recovering somewhat to close at 7852, down 80 on the day.

My T/A and P&F closed above 1 and was slightly higher. I am still looking for more separation between the bullish and bearish P&F before I have a better than moderate comfort level with trading. I have TWTR calls that have been on the negative side. So, looking forward to the morning earnings call to see if I gauged this correctly. The VIX remains tame and the treasury spread is about the same although the 10 and 2 both climbed higher. I'm also expecting some positive movement in USO and BOIL. NG storage is now dovetailing with the lower parameter of the 5-year average and much of the country remains above average temperature wise.

7/27/18

Well! Interesting how quickly all social media stocks have become pariahs! I can understand a 20% decline in FB because of the many recent missteps. Bot for TWTR to meet the street expectations and follow suit is goofy in my opinion. Twitter is after all ahead of the group in cleaning up its user base. The company should have been rewarded in my opinion for stepping up to the plate. The reaction today was irrational, again in my opinion. To now recap the day.

The S&P opened at 2842 (+5) but it was downhill from then on. An intraday low of 2808 (-29) was reached at around 1 pm but the index recovered somewhat to close at 2819, down 19. I am pleased to see there was no threat at falling to the 2800 area.

The Dow opened at 25521 (-6) and went on to hit an intraday high of 25580 (+53) at which point it reversed course to hit a low of 25370 (-157) before closing at 25451, down 76.

The Nas opened at 7890 (+38). It was all downhill from then on. It hit an intraday low of 7699 (-153) before closing at 7737, down 115.

The good news about today is that the VIX teased both its 50 and 200 Day SMA but closed at 13.00 below them. The VIX behavior today gives a trader comfort. My T/A and P&F sums ended below 1 but the P&F remained positive.

I took a bath on TWTR calls today and would like to see investors look at the positive results. I was expecting an upswing after they announced. This is how you learn, and I didn't unload.

7/30/18

It was an across the boards meltdown day. All indices were down and close to the day's low. The VIX closed up at 14.26, above its 50 Day SMA and just shy of its 200 Day SMA. My T/A and P&F closed below 1 and for the first time in several days the bull P&F was lower than the bear P&F.

The S&P opened even and rose to an intraday high of 2822 (+3) before dropping to an intraday low of 2798 (-21). It regained some of its loss to close at 2803, down 16.

The Dow opened at 25439 (-12) and reached an intraday high of 25500 (+49) before reversing direction to fall to a low of 25287 (-164). It too improved somewhat going into the close and ended at 25307, down 144.

The Nas opened at 7735 (-2) and reached 7740 (+3) but then turned negative to reach a low of 7604 (-133) before closing at 7630, down 107 on the day.

7/31/18

I'm starting to get a little concerned about the market direction for the immediate future after yesterday's and today's action. My biggest issue is with the P&F sums because the bear total is greater than the bull. Today, with the higher markets it should have been different. I sold much of my holdings including SPY. I just have a gut feeling that we might be repeating early February.

The S&P opened at 2810 (+7) and reached a high of 2824 (+21) before turning around to close at 2816, up 14.

The Dow opened at 25345 (+38) reaching an intraday high of 25491 (+184) before heading south to close at 25415, up 108.

The Nas opened at 7655 (+25) and hit an intraday low of 7615 (-15) before moving to an intraday high of 7709 (+79). Like the Dow and S&P it drifted lower toward the close to 7672, up 42.

The VIX closed at 12.81, a healthy drop from yesterday and below the 50 and 200 Day SMAs. But the PPO crossed its signal line. Need another day to confirm that the VIX is still benign. Both the NASDAQ and NYSE showed little interest in investing today. Maybe I'm a little paranoid!

8/01/18

Today's activity started off well but ended with the Nas staying positive.

The S&P opened at 2821 (+5) and rose to an intraday high of 2826 (+10) and a low of 2806 (-10) before closing at 2813, down 3.

The Dow opened at 25462 (+47) and shot to an intraday high of 25489 (+74) and then swan dived to a low of 25278 (-137) before recovering somewhat to close at 25334, down 81.

The Nas opened at 7702 (+30) and reached 7733 (+61) before falling to a low of 7671 and then recovering to close at 7707, up 35.

The VIX closed at 13.28 and my T/A And P&F sums ended below 1 for the third time in four days with the bear P&F sum still ahead of the bull sum.

8/02/18

The S&P opened at 2800 (-13) eventually falling to 2796 (-17) before turning around to hit an intraday high of 2830 (+17) before closing at 2827, up 14.

The Dow opened at 25256 (-78) and hit an intraday low of 25120 (-214) before reversing course to reach a high of 25360 (+26) and closed at 25326, down 8.

The Nas opened at 7660 (-47) and ran higher the rest of the session reaching an intraday high of 7809 (+102) before closing at 7803, up 96.

The VIX closed at 12.19 and my T/A and P&F sums closed below 1 again. Both T/A sums were higher than Wednesday by a decent percentage as was the bear sum for P&F. This doesn't happen often so I'm skittish when it comes to risk taking for now. NG supply broke below its running five-year low average, so I will assume that NG prices will move higher and will bet accordingly.

8/03/18

I really didn't expect the market to do well today, but it did. Indices are still moving sideways but then again this is August and the S&P is coming up against resistance. My T/A and P&F sums improved enough so that they are above 1, but there were only 2 times in the last six days that it has happened. Cash was negative for the NYSE and NASDAQ today. Because of these immediate trends I am more comfortable with being 50% invested at the close of this week. The VIX closed at 11.64 its lowest since around June 6. That means complacency is possibly setting in and worth keeping an eye pealed for any out of the ordinary change.

The S&P opened at 2830 (+3) and reached an intraday high of 2840 where it closed 13. It closed at its high for the day, something that hasn't been the norm of late.

The Dow opened at 25360 (+34) and reached an intraday high of 25468 (+142) before slacking off to close at 25463, up 136. That was just four points off the high.

The Nas opened at 7819 (+16) and struggled throughout the day. It hit a low of 7783 (-20) and a high of 7824 (+21) before closing at 7812, up 9.

8/06/18

The day was uneventful with the T/A and P&F sums staying above 1 for two days now and the VIX closing at 11.25. Cash was slightly negative on the NYSE going into the close.

The S&P opened at 2840 and reached an early low of 2836 (-4) and an intraday high of 2853 (+13) before scaling back to close at 2850, up 10. On January 29 it closed at 2854. The all-time high was 2873. So, it is possible to break new ground this week and possible to see the formation of a double top. At any rate there will be a lot of interest in the index I suspect.

The Dow opened at 25437 (-26) and reached an intraday low of 25381 (-82) and a high of 25540 (+77) before closing at 25502, up 40.

The Nas opened at 7810 (-2) and hit 7802 (-10) and a high intraday of 7860 at the close, up 48.

8/07/18

Today is one of those "I don't know what to think of today's market activity". On the immediate surface it looked like a good day for investors but the VIX dropped to 10.93 and my T/A and P&F sums all increased. This is unusual according to my spreadsheet because on a good day the bull side will increase while the bear side decreases. The sums were over 1 but less than yesterday's results. So, I remain cautious and am not fully invested.

The S&P opened at 2856 (+6) and achieved an intraday high of 2863 (+13) before closing at 2858, up 8.

The Dow opened at 25552 (+50) and hit an intraday high of 25693 (+191) and lost airspeed to close at 25629, up 127.

The Nas opened at 7879 (+19) and hit an intraday high of 7898 (+38) before closing at 7884, up 24.

All-in-all it was a good day but what that was for me a little discomforting because of my sums and the closes off of the intraday highs.

8/08/18

In the end it was a ho-hum kind'a day, a breather day. It was needed especially for the Dow because it has been steadily rising of late.

The S&P opened at 2857 (-1) and reached a high of 2862 (+4) and an intraday low of 2853 (-5) before closing at 2858, down 1, (rounding).

The Dow opened at 25617 (-12) and dropped to an intraday low of 25557 (-72) and a high of 25634 (+5) and closed at 25584, down 45.

The Nas opened at 7880 (-4) reaching a low of 7864 (-20) and a high of 7902 (+18) before closing at 7888, up 5.

The VIX is heading back to the "forget I am even here" location closing down at 10.81. It hasn't been at or below this level since mid-January. My T/A and P&F sums closed below 1. The P&F bull sum is higher than the bull sum, so I'll be keeping an eye on this. The dollar is growing stronger and oil is back down to 66.94. Natural Gas is now looking to break out from a line drawn from December 2016 and touching an early January high of this year. Tomorrow's EIA storage report will likely show it to remain below its five-year average.

8/09/18

I was expecting a less than stellar storage report from EIA but in fact it wasn't that bad although it ended up below the five-year average for a second week. So, I sold BOIL because of the nice runup over the last week. Anyway, trading seemed sluggish all day and there was very little movement.

The S&P opened at 2857 (-1) and hit allow of 2852 (-6) and a high of 2862 (+4) before closing at 2854, down 4.

The Dow opened at 25590 (+6) before hitting a high of 25613 (+29) and a low of 25493 (-91) before closing at 25509, down 75.

The Nas opened at 7887 (-1) and hit an intraday low of 7881 (-7) and a high of 7923 (+35) before closing at 7892, up 3. That's slightly below the July closing high of the 25th.

The VIX rose during the day and closed at 11.25. My T/A and P&F ended above 1 with both bull sums ahead of the bear sums. That made me feel better.

8/10/18

There are good days and bad days when you are watching your stocks performance. Today was one of the latter. All indices lost about three-quarters of a percent except the Russell. The VIX closed at 13.16 for a 1.89-point increase and at exactly its 50 Day SMA. My T/A and P&F sums ended up well below 1 and cash was negative for both the NYSE and NASDAQ. Blame for today's rout was Turkey's dramatic caving of its Lire. So, time for today's results.

The S&P opened at 2840 (-14) and reached an intraday low of 2826 (-28) before closing at 2833, down 20.

The Dow opened at 25401 (-108) and hit an intraday low of 25223 (-286) before closing at 25313, down 196.

The Nas opened at 7835 (-57) and reached an intraday low of 7818 (-74) before closing at 7839, down 53.

I'm still expecting an attempt at a new high for the S&P and today's turnover might well be the minor adjustment needed.

8/13/18

Back to back bad days. The percent decline was not as bad as Friday and the guilty party remains the Turkish Lire which collapsed further. The day started off okay, but it didn't take very long to fall into disrepair.

The S&P opened at 2835 (+2) and reached a high of 2843 (+10) but started downhill at around 1100 hr. reaching 2820 (-13) before closing at 2822, down 11.

The Dow opened at 25327 (+14) hitting a high of 25381 (+68) before heading down to reach an intraday low of 25154 (-159) before recovering somewhat to close at 25188, down 125.

The Nas opened at 7848 (+9) hitting an intraday high of 7889 (+50) and a low of 7814 (-25) before closing at 7820, down 19.

The VIX closed at 14.75, moving above both its 50 and 200 Day SMA. My T/A and P&F sums are below 1 for the third time in five days. It's unusual to see this happen so I am expecting improvements now. I also consider the fact that many traders take time off in August and this enhances volatility, especially with a global event such as a Turkish Lire bath. Of course, I hope I'm right!

8/14/18

Things were improved today. The indices were all up and the VIX relaxed as well and ranged between 14.22 and 13.11, closing at 13.34. That put it back below its 200 Day SMA. My T/A and P&F sums increased but remained below 1. The NYSE and NASDAQ were both slightly cash positive.

The S&P opened at 2828 (+6) and reached a high of 2843 (+21) closing at 2840, up 18.

The Dow opened at 25216 (+28) briefly touched a high of 25340 (+152) before closing at 25300, up 112.

The Nas opened at 7848 (+28) and hit an intraday high of 7878 (+58) closing at 7872, up 51.

All indices have been closing above their SMA with enough cushion.

I don't expect any easy moves up now, especially after reviewing a couple of forward-looking videos by presenters for Chartcon2018. They agree that between now and the middle of September will likely be a volatile period after which things should improve.

8/15/18

One of the speakers at Chartcon2018 predicted the correction that we are now in the throes of. I subscribed to it so that I could listen to the presenters at my leisure. I also have links to the PP presentations that they followed. After just listening to the first three I have already learned much in the way of risk avoidance.

Today was a down day but so far, the Dow is closing above 25000 and the S&P above 2802. These values should prove support, but we'll see if that's the case tomorrow. The VIX jumped to 16.86 at one point today but closed at 14.66. That's above both SMAs. My T/A and P&F sums were below 1 at .40. The last time I saw similar values was in June.

The S&P opened at 2828 (-12) and dropped to 2802 (-38) intraday and then closed at 2818, down 22.

The Dow opened at 25235 (-65) and dipped to 24966 (-334) before recovering somewhat to close at 25162, down 138.

The Nas opened at 7810 (-61) and reached an intraday low of 7733 (-138) before recovering to 7774, down 97.

8/16/18

The indices did very well today recovering from yesterday's losses and then some.

The S&P opened at 2831 (+13) and reached an intraday high of 2850 (+32) before closing at 2841, up 23.

The Dow opened at 25295 (+133) and hit an intraday high of 25607 (+445) before closing at 25559, up 397.

The Nas opened at 7827 (+53) and reached an intraday high of 7850 (+76) before closing at 7807, up 33.

The VIX closed at 13.45, down 1.21. My T/A and P&F sums were above 1 at market close.

8/17/18

Today was a pleasant end of the week close during this manic/depressive week. The indices closed higher after a stellar day yesterday and the VIX relaxed below its 50 and 200 Day SMAs once more at 12.64. My T/A and S&P sums closed above 1 and that tells me we the market is in bull mode again. The P&F bear sum is still higher than the bull sum but better than yesterday's result.

The S&P opened at 2838 (-3) and reached a low of 2834 (-7) early and rose throughout the day hitting a high of 2856 (+15) before closing at 2850, up 9. This index is 23 points away from its all-time high. Will it move in on it next week or shy away again?

The Dow opened at 25551 (-8) and hit an intraday low of 25522 (-37) and later reached a high of 25728 (+169) before closing at 25669, up 111. It is 948 points away from its all-time high or 3.6%.

The Nas opened at 7787 (-20) and reached a low of 7753 (-54) and a high of 7831 (+24) before closing at 7816, up 10. I expect more sideways movement before another run at a new high with this index.

8/20/18

Today was another positive day across all indices. The VIX was lower closing at 12.48 and my T/A and P&F sums improved. The only fly in the ointment was that the indices all closed below the highs of the day.

The S&P opened at 2854 (+4) and reached 2860 (+10) intraday before closing at 2857, up 7.

The Dow opened at 25728 (+59 and reached 25790 (+121) before losing some steam to close at 25759, up 89.

The Nas opened at 7834 (+18) and it a low of 7788 (-28) and a high of 7837 (+21) before closing at 7821, up 5.

There are trade talks going on in D.C. with a Chinese contingent. That lead to some of today's optimism and yet traders didn't want to be exposed overnight apparently which was demonstrated at the end of the session. Having said that any day that closes higher than the previous is a good day.

8/21/18

The S&P hit a new all-time high of 2873 (2873.23) and retreated. The previous high of 2872.87 was registered on January 26. Now this could spell a double top or a new run up. I'm betting on the latter although it may not occur until September. The S&P started falling when CNBC announced that the President's former attorney, Michael Cohen, had agreed to a plea deal to include 3 to 5 years of prison time. Because the CNBC talking heads keep looking for that one piece of evidence that will spell curtains for Mr. Trump, I believe the discussion torpedoed a good rally attempt. Just my opinion.

All indices closed higher as did the VIX. It closed at 12.82. My T/A and P&F closed over 2 for the first time since July 9. It wasn't that uncommon in December and January for a close over 2. So, we could be in for a nice rally similar to that period. The remaining index that needs to hit a new high is the Dow.

The S&P opened at 2862 (+5) and hit a new intraday high of 2873 before closing at 2863, up 6.

The Dow opened at 25787 (+28) and achieved a high of 25889 (+130) before losing ground to close at 25822, up 64.

The Nas opened at 7840 (+19) and reached 7898 (+77) before closing at 7859, up 38.

8/22/18

With today's market close this bull market became the longest running one in history. It was not a spectacular day at all. The S&P closed fractionally down, the Dow closed down 89 points and the Nas closed up 30. My T/A and P&F sums were over 1 and the bull P&F sums were higher than the bear sums for two days in a row now. The VIX closed down at 12.23 although it had reached a high of 13.29 intraday. Given the political picture with Manafort and Cohen's convictions it could have been a much worse day.

The S&P opened at 2861 (-1) and hit a low of 2856 (-7) and a high of 2868 (+5) before closing at 2862, down 1.

The Dow opened at 25825 (+3) and reached a high of 25836 (+14) before struggling the rest of the day. It hit an intraday low of 25722 (-100) before closing off its low at 25734, down 89.

The Nas opened at 7844 (-15) and reached an intraday low of 7841 (-18) and a high of 7898 (+39) before closing at 7889, up 30.

8/23/18

Today we are celebrating 32 years of marriage. A nice milestone to enjoy.

On the other hand, the market was a lackluster event. But given the recent political news and nice moves up these last few weeks it is certainly understandable and not unexpected.

The S&P opened at 2860 (-2) and reached an intraday high of 2869 (+7) and a low of 2854 (-8) before closing at 2857, up 5.

The Dow opened at 25715 (-19) and reached 25763 (+29) before putting it in reverse to hit 25608 (-126) intraday and ended the session at 25657, up 77.

The Nas opened at 7886 (-3) and hit an intraday low of 7867 (-22) and a high of 7926 (+37) before losing ground to close at 7878, down 11.

My T/A and P&F sums remained over 1 and the P&F sums actually improved despite the day's results. This tells me that there is a lot of potential for an improving market that is now the longest bull market in our history.

8/24/18

The Nasdaq and S&P registered new highs today and closed at new highs as well. Pretty good considering that it was a Friday and nothing to report concerning any favorable news with respect to trade and tariffs during ongoing negotiations. Pompeo is not going to Korea on a scheduled trip either because it is reported that "Rocket Man" isn't following up on previous negotiations. The VIX closed down at 11.99 and my T/A and P&F sums remained above 1.

The S&P opened at 2862 (+5) and reached an intraday high of 2876 (+19) and closed at 2875, up 18.

The Dow opened at 25689 (+32) and climbed to 25826 (+169) intraday, closing at 25790, up 133.

The Nas opened at 7908 (+30) and rose to 7950 (+72) before closing at 7946, up 68.

I was a little concerned that the bull P&F dropped 1 point while the bear P&F rose 19, given that new highs were reached today. This may not mean anything, but I will keep an eye out.

8/27/18

The S&P, Nas and Russell 2000 (I don't comment on) all hit new highs and closed at new highs today and the Dow closed above 26000. Pretty good day for traders! The VIX closed at 12.14, slightly higher and My T/A and P&F sums were over 2. There is finally a nice spread between the bull and bear P&F sums as well.

The S&P opened at 2885 (+10) and hit a new intraday high of 2898 (+23) and closed at 2897, up 22.

The Dow opened up at 25883 (+93) and reached an intraday high of 26068 (+278) and closed at 26050, up 259 on the day.

The Nas opened at 7990 (+44) and hit a new intraday high of 8025 (+79) before closing at 8018, up 72.

I am hoping that we continue this good run through Friday because September is generally not a stellar month for stocks. I will be on the lookout for weakness in any stocks we own.

8/28/18

Today was a day of rest and reflection for the market. Nothing much really happened. Siesta time due to the heat wave.

The S&P opened at 2901 (+4) and hit a high of 2904 (+7) and a low of 2894 (-3) before closing at 2898, up 1.

The Dow opened at 26093 (+43) and hit a high of 26122 (+72) and an intraday low of 26038 (-12) before closing at 26064, up 14.

The Nas opened at 8039 (+21) and hit a high of 8046 (+28) and a low of 8010 (-8) before closing at 8030, up 12.

8/29/18

The S&P, Nas and Russell 2000 all hit new all-time highs and new closing highs today and the Dow intraday high was just 449 points short of its all-time high! It was a respectable day for all of the major indices. The VIX barely moved closing at 12.26 and my T/A and P&F sums were well above 1.

The S&P opened at 2901 (+3) and reached 2916 (+18) before closing at 2914, up 16.

The Dow opened at 26083 (+19) and reached an intraday high of (+104) after a short sell-off to 26035

(-29). It closed at 26125, up 61.

The Nas opened at 8044 (+14) and reached an intraday high of 8114 (+84) before closing at 8110, up 80.

This month is turning out to be a good one which is a little unusual because most months of August are more geared to doing nothing.

8/30/18

If you want to be something really scary for Halloween dress up like a tariff!

The markets were basically digesting recent gains when someone yelled "tariff" at around 3:00 pm. It was as effective as yelling fire in a crowded theater because the indices all took a header and ended lower on the day. The VIX rose to 13.95 before backing off to 13.51, closing above its 50 Day SMA. My T/A and P&F sums changed little and remained well above 1.

The S&P opened at 2909 (-5) and reached an intraday low of 2895 (-19) before recovering somewhat to close at 2901, down 13. Glad to see that it closed above 2900.

The Dow opened at 26099 (-26) and hit an intraday low of 25935 (-190) before recovering to 25987, down 138.

The Nas opened at 8094 (-16) and climbed to 8133 (+23) pre-tariff news and then nosed down to 8070

(-40) before recovering to close at 8088, down 21.

Quite an afternoon to say the least. Let's hope tomorrow doesn't follow suit.

8/31/18

Another month and week gone as we head into September.

Not much to talk about concerning today's activities. Traders were looking for some positive news regarding a trade agreement with Canada but, by the close there was no news. After being down most of the day the indices basically ended flat with only the Nas and gaining ground.

The S&P opened at 2898 (-3) and managed a high of 2906 (+5) and an intraday low of 2892 (-9) before closing at 2902, up 1.

The Dow opened at 25965 (-22) and hit an intraday high of 26029 (+42) and a low of 25880 (-107) before crawling back to close at 2595, up 22.

The Nas was the exception opening at 8079 (-9) and then moved up to a high of 8120 (+32) before closing at 8110, up 21.

The VIX closed at 12.90 and my T/A and P&F sums remained above 1.

September

9/04/18

Down to the final four…months of the year that is.

The market was pretty negative given that there was no bad news over the long weekend. Must be panic from traders realizing that they are in September, the worst month of the year for stocks in general. Of course, August is usually no great shakes either but, it turned out nicely. Of interest was Amazon's temporarily hitting the trillion mark, the second company to do so.

The VIX showed some signs of life rising to 14.35 before closing at 13.16. That's below its 50 Day SMA but close to both moving averages. My T/A and P&F sums closed below 1 as well.

The S&P opened at 2897 (-5) and hit an intraday low of 2885 (-17) before recovering to where it opened at 2897, down 5.

The Dow opened at 25916 (-49) and managed a low of 25806 (-159) but recovered to close at 25952, down 12.

The Nas opened at its prior close of 8088 and hit a morning high of 8104 (+16) before reversing course to register a low of 8042 (-46). It too recovered somewhat to close at 8091, down 18.

9/05/18

Not a fun day to be long. The markets were negative for most of the day with only the Dow closing up. The VIX rose to 14.30 and dropped some to close at 13.91. that puts it between its 50 and 200 Day SMA.

My T/A and P&F sums remain below 1 with both bear sums ahead of their bull sums.

The S&P opened at 2892 (-5) and reached a low of 2877 (-20) early and gradually recovered to close at 2889, down 8.

The Dow opened at 25920 (-32) and dropped to an early morning low of 25871 (-81) and reached a high of 26011 (+59) before closing at 25975, up 23.

The Nas opened at 8074 (-17) and reached a low of 7962 (-129) before struggling to close at 7995, down 96. Cash was negative all day on the NASDAQ and slightly positive on the NYSE. Nothing to get concerned about.

9/06/18

Another negative day except for the Dow. There were no knockout punches, just constant bruising of the Nas and S&P. The VIX closed at 14.63, slightly below its 200 Day SMA. It is forming a reverse head and

shoulder which of course I hope is a false signal. My T/A and P&F sums were a little more bullish but ended below 1.

The S&P opened at yesterday's close of 2889, reaching a high of 2892 (+3) and a low of 2867 (-22) before closing at 2878, down 11.

The Dow opened at 25973 (-2) and reached a high of 26074 (+99) and a low of 25881 (-94) before closing at 25996, up 21.

The Nas has been the worst performer all week after its recent runup to record highs. It opened at 7998

(+3) and reached a high of 8002 (+7) and an intraday low of 7885 (-110) before closing at 7923, down 72.

Will things turn around tomorrow?

9/07/18

September is living up to its notoriety so far. The indices all ended down while the VIX closed above its 200 Day SMA and the reverse H&S is still in play. It close at 14.88 and had been as high as 15.63. The T/A and P&F sums were below 1 for the 4th day in a row. Should it continue I am willing to say that we will see another correction. Next week will be interesting.

The S&P opened at 2868 (-10) and reached a high of 2884 (+6) and a low of 2864 (-14) before recovering somewhat to close at 2872, down 6.

The Dow opened at 25951 (-45) but moved higher to 26003 (+7) and then to an intraday low of 25818

(-178) before closing at 25917, down 79.

The Nas opened at 7879 (-44) and moved to a morning high of 7963 (+40) and a low of 7874 (-49) before closing at 7903, down 20.

9/10/18

Two things concern me after today. The first one is that today's T/A and P&F sums results of less than 1 is now on day 5. The second is that the P&F bear sums compared to the bull sums were worse than Friday even though the T/A sums closed in the opposite direction. The VIX did close at 14.18 and back below its 200 Day SMA. All-in-all it was a lackluster day.

The S&P opened at 2881 (+9) and hit a high of 2887 (+15) and closed at 2877, up 5.

The Dow looked very promising at the open with an open of 25992 (+75). It then reached a high of 26040 (+123) but lost that velocity throughout the day. It reached an intraday low of 25854 (-63) before closing at 25857, down 59.

The Nas opened at 7940 (Friday's close) and hit a high of 7945 (+37) and a low of 7890 (-13) and closed at 7924, up 22.

9/11/08

17-year anniversary of the day that we as a Country were again attacked. Wall Street continues to acknowledge it with a moment of silence at the opening bell.

Today saw improvement in the market as the major indices closed higher. The VIX closed at 13.21 and my T/A and P&F sums remained below 1 for the 6th day in a row.

The S&P opened at 2872 (-5) and hit a low of 2867 (-10) and a high of 2893 (+16) before closing at 2888, up 11.

The Dow opened at 25841 (-16) and reached an intraday low of 25754 (-103) and a high of 26020 (+163)

before closing at 25971, up 114.

The Nas opened at 7895 (-29) and dropped to a low of 7881 (-43) and reached a high of 7986 (+62) before closing at 7927, up 48.

The market remains unsettled in my opinion and I am therefore mostly cash. Time will tell when the market settles into a more bullish or bearish mode because it seems it could go either way over the next few days.

9/12/18

The S&P opened at 2888 which was the previous close. It reached an intraday low of 2879 (-9) and a high of 2895 (+7) and then closed at 2889, up 1.

The Dow opened at 25989 (+18) and reached a low of 25929 (-42) and a high of 26146 (+175) before closing at 25999, up 28.

The Nas opened at 7959 (-13) and hit a low of 7884 (-88) and closed at 7954, down 18.

There is obviously an air of uncertainty about the market's direction given the extremes of the Dow and Nas. The VIX did slack off to 13.14 and my T/A and P&F remained below 1 for the 7th day.

9/13/18

Today was a good day for the markets. The VIX fell a little to 12.34 which puts it below both moving averages and my T/A and P&F sums registered above 1 for a change. I would have been happier to see some better movement with the P&F sums but accept the result as positive.

The S&P opened at 2897 (+8) and hit a high of 2907 (+18) before closing at 2904, up 15.

The Dow opened at 26084 (+85) and reached an intraday high of 26192 (+193) before closing at 26146, up 147.

The Nas opened at 8000 (+46) and reached an intraday high of 8038 (+84) before closing at 8014, up 59.

9/14/18

Today was a typical Friday of late. The markets opened slightly higher and then hit a selling wall and spent the afternoon recovering to close near yesterday's close. My T/A and P&F sums were again over 1 but only by a fingernail. There was improvement with the P&F sums variance but not enough to flip it bullish favored. The VIX slipped a little further to 12.10 and cash in/out of the NYSE and Nasdaq was basically neutral. I closed out some trades and am now 0nly 21% in equities. I would consider this a tiring week and after reviewing several options for trading I was simply not comfortable with being much longer over the weekend.

Of interest too were recent StockCharts.com blogs. Although they come across in their conclusions as remaining bullish, there is not very much gusto behind the comments. The Doom and Gloom crowd is also getting more play on CNBC, not that

I pay that much attention to it. Just saying! Sometimes you just wake up in the middle of the night with an uncomfortable feeling about the market. I'm sure most traders do. It's just a feeling that things are going to turn, and I never want to be on the wrong side. That is where I am now. Of course, Monday can change that!

The S&P opened at 2906 (+2) and hit a high of 2908 (+4) and a low of 2896 (-8) and closed at 2905, up 1.

The Dow opened at 26170 (+24) and reached a high of 26211 (+65) and a low of 26068 (-78) before closing at 26155, up 9.

The Nas opened at 8026 (+12) and hit a high of 8041 (+27) and allow of 7980 (-34), closing at 8010, down 4.

9/17/18

True to history the markets slumped again. Tariff threats geared to China of another $200 billion didn't help nor did the last-minute shenanigans of the Kavanaugh hearings. The VIX closed up at 13.68. That once again puts it above its 50 Day SMA but well below its 200 Day SMA.

The S&P opened at 2904 (-1) and hit a low of 2886 (-19) during the last hour of trading and closed at 2889, down 16.

The Dow opened at 26152 (-3) and managed an early high of 26184 (+29) but then careened on down the road to a low of 26030 (-125) before closing at 26062, down 93.

The Nas suffered the most opening at 7992 (-18) and reached a low of 7890 (-120) before closing at 7896, down 114.

9/18/18

The markets regained some of yesterday's losses and the Dow did better. Again, using tariff as an excuse because those imposed were 10% instead of the full 25% promised by year end against Chinese goods. The VIX ended lower at 12.79 and at its 50 Day SMA. My T/A and P&F sums remain below 1 and I found it interesting that the bullish T/A was almost equal to the bearish sums, but the P&F sums decreased on the bullish side while the sums increased on the bearish side. Then again, only the Dow recovered yesterday's losses.

The S&P opened at 2891 (+2) and rose to a high of 2911 (+22) before closing at 2904, up 16.

The Dow opened at 26076 (+14) and reached a high of 26317 (+255) before closing at 26247, up 185.

The Nas opened at 7904 (+8) and shot to a high of 7986 (+90) before closing at 7956, up 60.

So, not a bad day!

9/19/18

If you were just watching the Dow, you'd believe that the markets are doing well. You need to look at the other indices as well and you'll see the true picture. The S&P is attempting a new high but shies away and the Nas is still well behind Friday's close of 8010. The Russell is below its all-time high of 1742 as well. My T/A and P&F

sums continue to erode as well. The sums have been above 1 on only 2 of the last twelve days and yet the VIX remains complacent closing at 11.77 today. I wouldn't be surprised to see a 1 or 2 % drop in the majors by COB Friday and am 25% inequities of which most is GE that I felt comfortable buying today based on my charts.

The S&P opened at 2907 (+3) and hit a high of 2912 before closing at 2908, up 4.

The Dow opened at 26288 (+41) and climbed to 26464 (+217) before closing at 26406, up 159. It is just 211 points from its all-time high of 26617 recorded on Jan. 26.

The Nas opened at 7963 (+7) and reached an intraday high of 7976 (+20) and a low of 7918 (-38 before closing at 7950, down 6.

Tomorrow should be interesting (or Not).

9/20/18

All of the major indices closed higher today. The S&P hit a new intraday high of 2935 (+27) after opening at 2920 (+12) and closed just a few points below it at 2931, up 23.

The Dow did, likewise, hitting a new intraday high of 26698 (+292) after opening at 26519 (+113). It closed at 26657, up 251.

The Nas opened at 7994 (+44) and reached a high of 8039 (+89) before closing at 8028, up 78.

The VIX closed slightly higher on the day at 11.89. It ended with a candlestick hammer. This suggests that it might close higher tomorrow.

My T/A sums were significantly improved and the P&F sums only somewhat. It did close above 1 for a change but that is now 3 of 13 days.

I hope this trend continues but I need to see a greater participation in bullish T/A and P&F sums before I feel strongly about being invested heavily overnight. My GE buy hit a snag right from the get-go due to a reported turbine failure on an HA unit.

9/21/18

The Dow and S&P both hit new intraday highs today. Problem is that the rest of the indices haven't followed suit. The Nas and Russell 2000 both closed lower and account for a much greater number of stocks under their umbrella. My T/A bull sums dropped, and the bear sums greatly increased. The P&F bull sums increased but the bear sums increased at a higher percentage leading to another day less than 1. That makes 3 positive closes out of 14 days. The VIX closed at 11.60, slightly down from yesterday.

The S&P opened at 2937 (+6) and reached a new intraday high of 2941 (+10) and a low of 2927 (-4) before closing at 2930, down 1.

The Dow opened at 26726 (+69) and hit a new intraday high of 26769 (+112) and closed at 26743, up 87.

The Nas opened at 8041 (+13) and managed an early high of 8057 (+29) and then began a slide to 7980 (-48) before closing at 7987, down 41.

And yes, GE dipped some more today and on higher volume than yesterday which was already higher than normal.

9/24/18

It was a Monday and most indices were down. However, the VIX barely rose and there was improvement with the P&F sums. The bullish sum was higher than Friday while the bearish sum was actually lower than Friday. When added with the T/A sums the result was less than 1. Maybe there is a turnaround coming.

The S&P opened at 2922 (-8) and hit an intraday low of 2913 (-17) before closing at 2919, down 11.

The Dow opened at 26705 (-38) and dropped to 26549 (-194) intraday before closing at 26562, down 181.

The Nas opened at 7939 (-48) and reached a low of 7912 (-75) before recovering to hit a high of 7998

(+11) and then closed at 7993, up 6.

9/25/18

The indices opened higher and the day looked positive until around mid-day. At that point the S&P and Dow started selling off, closing down for the day. The VIX ended up at 12.47 and my T/A and P&F sums remained below 1.

The S&P opened at 2922 (+3) and reached a high of 2924 (+5) and a low of 2914 (-5) before closing at 2916, down 4.

The Dow opened at 26602 (+40) and hit a high of 26635 (+73) and a low of 26476 (-86) and closed at 26492, down 70.

The Nas opened at 8002 (+9) and fell to an intraday low of 7979 (-14) and a high of 8014 (+21) before closing at 8007, up 14.

9/26/18

The markets do not like uncertainty and something definitely spooked traders at around 3:00. The catalyst according to CNBC was the report that the FED expects a growth rate of around 3% and that it is not concerned about inflation. I also believe the uncertainty around the coming theatrics with respect to Judge Kavanaugh has something to do with it as well.

The VIX closed at 12.88 (+.46) and that was above its 50 Day SMA. My T/A and P&F sums were below 1. This means only 3 of the last 17 days closed favorably. So, my concerns for the future few weeks are growing. Day trading seems to be the only safe approach to be in the market and you need to be acutely alert with how the trades are doing, IMO.

The S&P opened at 2917 (+1) and managed a high of 2931 (+15) before dropping to an intraday low of

2903 (-13) before closing at 2906, down 10.

The Dow opened at 26537 (+45) and hit a high of 26606 (+114) before reversing gears to close at 26385, down 107. It hit an intraday low of 26349 (-143).

The Nas likewise opened up at 8012 (+5) and reached 8067 (+60) and a low of 7983 (-24) before closing at 7990, down 17.

9/27/18

The indices closed higher, the VIX was down to 12.41 but I remain uncomfortable about where the market may be heading in the near future because my T/A and P&F sums remain below 1 for 3 out of 18 days.

The S&P opened at 2912 (+6) and reached a high of 2927 (+21) before closing 2914, up 8.

The Dow opened at 26418 (+33) and did hit a low of 26380 (-5) and an intraday high of 26557 (+172) before closing at 26440, up 55.

The Nas opened at 8021 (+31) and hit a high of 8072 (+82) before closing at 8042, up 52.

Maybe it is a September or the FED or trader anxiety, but the markets are showing weakness. It is clear to me that the markets can tip either way. As I mentioned yesterday the only way, I'm comfortable trading is by keeping a constant eye on my buys.

9/28/18

Today was the last trading day of the week, month and quarter. The S&P was the only index that closed down and that was by two cents. Here are my two cents thanks to Creedence Clearwater Revival; "I see the bad moon rising, I see trouble on the way."

The good news is that the VIX closed down at 12.12. The bad news is that my T/A and P&F sums remain below 1, now for 3 of 19 days. The bull T/A sum rose but so did the bear sum. The bull P&F dropped again while the bear sum rose. T/A new 52-week highs were 217 and new lows 501. I am looking for a healthy correction, sooner than later and I could be wrong, but I am still keeping a low profile by remaining at 74% cash. My two largest holdings are BOIL and XLU.

The S&P opened at 2910 (-4) and managed a low of 2908 (-6) before turning up to reach a high of 2921

(+7) before closing at yesterday's close of 2914.

The Dow opened at 26408 (-32) and hit a low of 26384 (-56) and a high of 26516 (+76), closing at 26458, up 18.

The Nas also opened lower at 8024 (-18) and dropped to a low of 8016 (-26) and a high of 8065 (+23). It closed at 8046, up 4.

October

10/01/18

The market took off like gang-busters because of the announcement that Canada and the U.S. had come to terms as trading partners. That being said, the S&P and Dow closed higher while the Nas and Russell closed down. I expected to see some improvement with my T/A and P&F sums but the bull sums and bear sums both increased keeping the ratio below 1. That's now for 3 of 20 days. The VIX remained unchanged.

The S&P opened at 2926 (+12) and reached a high of 2937 (+23) early and closed at 2925, up 11.

The Dow opened at 26598 (+140) and reached a high of 26738 (+280) before closing at 29951, up 193.

The Nas opened at 8092 (+46) and reached a high of 8107 (+61) and then went downhill from the early morning rush to a low of 8020 (-26) before closing at 8037, down 9.

Each of these indices remained below the previous all-time highs intraday even though it looked early on like they might be challenged. Maybe tomorrow.

10/02/18

The Dow did well today but it was the only index to do so. The S&P was positive for most of the day and the Nas for only an hour or so in the late morning. The VIX is at 12.05 but my T/A and P&F sums continue to get worse which simply shows that most stocks are on a losing streak with the exceptions of those in the Dow, Nas and S&P. My sums are now at 3 of 21 trading days. I keep looking for some kind of correction, but nothing is forecasting such an event.

The S&P opened at 2924 (-1) and reached a low of 2919 (-6) and a high of 2931 (+6), closing at 2923, down 2 (rounding).

The Dow opened at 26649 (-2) and hit an early low of 26628 (-23) and a new intraday all-time high of 26825 (+174) before closing at 26774, up 123 on the day.

The Nas opened at 8024 (-13) and reached a high of 8054 (+17) and an intraday low of 7984 (-53) before closing at 8000, down 38 (rounding).

All of the indices have now reached new highs since January, the Dow being the laggard. Hopefully, we aren't double topping.

10/03/18

The sky hasn't fallen yet but, only the Dow is really cranking now. The VIX is a non-starter for now falling to 11.63 and my T/A and P&F sums remain below 1. However, they did improve today with bullish sums improving and the bearish sums falling.

As has been the recent scenario, the S&P opened at 2932 (+9) and hit an intraday high of 2940 (+17), almost hitting the recent all-time high. It shifted direction at about

2:15 when the Emergency Alert test ran and must have thrown some fear into traders because all of the indices headed south with the S&P hitting a low of 2921 (-2) before recovering to close at 2926, up 2 (rounding).

The Dow opened at 26833 (+59) and reached a new intraday high of 26952 (+178) before closing at 26828, up 54.

The Nas opened at 8035 (+35) and reached a high of 8054 (+54) before closing at 8025, up 26. (rounding).

10/04/18

We got a small correction today. Not sure that it was enough to settle some dust, but we'll see. The VIX closed above its 50 Day SMA and my T/A and P&F sums really took a hit.

The S&P opened at 2919 (-7) and eventually hit a low of 2884 (-42) before closing at 2902, down 24.

The Dow opened at 26784 (-44) and reached its low of 26472 (-356) before regaining some of its loss to close at 26627, down 201.

The Nas took a 2.4% hit intraday after opening at 7993 (-32). It hit a low of 7833 (-192) before recovering to 7880, down 146 (1.81%). The last time it closed that low was August 23.

10/05/18

Today was another correction day. The VIX hit a high of 17.36 before settling at 14.98. It closed above its 50 and 200 Day SMAs. As for my T/A and P&F sums I am breaking them down for this iteration. Today's T/A bull sum was 1212. The last time that it was that low was March 23. The T/A bear sum was 6092 yesterday and 5055 today. The T/A bear sum was 6092 yesterday and 5055 today. The last time that it was this high consecutively was February 5/6, 2018. The P&F bull sum was 1004 today. The last time it was that low was April 4, 2018 when it ended the day at 958. The P&F bear sum was 2134. The last time that it was that high was February 6, 2018. The point that I am trying to present is that the sums from the last 24 days have been less than 1 on 21 of those trading days. This simply is a different spin on the advance/decline presentation and the last two trading days are simply helping to validate conclusions I make based on the number of days above 1, which is breakeven.

The S&P opened at 2903 (+1) and ran up to 2910 (+8) before changing direction to reach a low of 2869 (-33). It regained enough to close at 2886, down 16. It was briefly below its 50 Day SMA of 2877. Will it hold?

The Dow opened at 26633 (+6) and did hit an intraday high of 26676 (+49) before dropping to 26302 (-325) during the day. It recovered some to close at 26447, down 180.

The Nas opened at 7875 (-5) and rose to 7903 (+23) intraday. This index hit a low of 7716 (-164) before recovering to close at 7788, down 91. It closed below its 50 Day SMA of 7919. This index has had a very tough drop of 237 (2.95%) points since Wednesday's close of 8025.

10/08/18

The VIX rose from the start of trading hitting a high of 18.38, then reversing direction to close at 15.81. It remained above both its 50 and 200 Day SMAs but formed a shooting star pattern which could be indicative of a reversal. The next day or two will determine this. My T/A and P&F sums remain bearish and in the case of the P&F sums are in an even more negative position. The indices were all over the place today with the Dow being the only one ending up.

The S&P opened at 2878 (-8) and hit an intraday low of 2862 (-24) and a high of 2889 (+3) before closing at 2884, down 2 (rounding).

The Dow opened at 26399 (-48) and reached a low of 26223 (-224) and a high of 26529 (+82) and then closed at 26487, up 40.

The Nas opened at 7747 (-41) and moved as low as 7655 (-133) after briefly reaching a high of 7797

(+9) before closing at 7736, down 52.

Today was Columbus Day or Indigenous Peoples Day and the end of a three-day weekend for some. Tomorrow will be a much more interesting day.

10/09/18

Today was like yesterday with just more confusion. All indices pointed down with the exception of the Nas and later on all were in the green. The morning was reasonably promising but that didn't last long. The Dow and S&P ended in the red with the Nas holding green by a whisker. The VIX was at 17.49 but at no time a threat of breaking out. It closed at 15.95, .25 higher than yesterday.

The S&P opened at 2882 (-2) and hit an intraday high of 2895 (+11) and a low of 2874 (-10) before closing at 2880, down 4.

The Dow opened at 26469 (-18) and hit a low early of 26324 (-163) and went on to a high of 26540 (+53) and then was up and down throughout the day to close at 26431, down 56.

The Nas opened at 7729 (-7) and hit a low of 7719 (-17) and a high of 7800 (+64) before closing at 7738, up 2.

All-in-all, the day seemed promising at about 10:30. I even bought some SPY near its high but sold it (at a minor loss) at around 3:30 because the indices have become pretty predictable with respect to the final 30 minutes of trading.

10/10/18

Where do you start a narration about a day like today? If you were invested, you likely felt panicky. If you were mostly cash, you likely sighed with relief. The key numbers at the end of the day are the VIX closed at 22.79, the S&P lost 94 (-3.29%), The Dow lost 832 (-3.15%) and the Nas lost 316 (-4.08%). Needless to say, my T/A and P&F sums were down and closed at .19. The last time it was anywhere near there was March 23 when it was 20. If you are looking for good news, the Sox beat the Yankees last night and are in the ALCS playoffs.

The S&P opened at 2874 (-6) and it was downhill from there on. The low was 2785 (-95) and the close was 2786, down 94.

The Dow opened at 26442 (+11) and skidded to a low of 25594 (-837) and closed at 25599, down 832.

The Nas opened at 7693 (-44) and free fell to 7421 (-317) and closed at 7422, down 316. Just a week ago the Nas hit an intraday high of 8054. The difference between that high and today's close is 632 points and a drop of 7.8%. The difference between today's close and its all-time high of 8133 is 8.7%.

10/11/18

I have kept the T/A and P&F sums spreadsheet since 3/21/16, when I retired because I was looking for something to do to keep my 10-key skills. It is no hardship to sum the corporations included in each scan. Today the bull P&F scans sum was 699. Reviewing the spreadsheet, I found the last lowest total to be 825 on March 23 of this year. Today's entry of 699 established a new low of the P&F bull sums. Today's bear P&F sum was 2829. I did have a higher reading once before on February 6 of this year. It was 2937. So, my overall concern is that we will be seeing a correction that was greater than the one this spring, based on these numbers.

The S&P opened at 2777 (-9) and rose to an intraday high of 2795 (+9) and a low of 2711 (-75) before closing at 2728, down 58.

The Dow opened at 25518 (-81) and managed an intraday high of 25684 (+85) and hit a low of 24900 (-699) before closing at 25053, down 546.

The Nas opened at 7388 (-34) hitting 7493 (+71) before sliding to a low of 7274 (-148) before closing off its low at 7329, down 93.

The Nas is now down 804 from its all-time high of 88133 or 10%. The Dow hit an intraday high of 26952 on October 3, 1918. It is down 1899 points or 7%. The S&P hit its all-time high of 2941 on September 21. It closed down 213 points from its all-time high or 7.2%.

Because a Friday is the next trading day, I don't expect the Dow or S&P to go positive. Because 10% is sometimes the magic number for a correction we could see the Nas at least stabilize during tomorrow's trading.

10/12/18

Today was a rally day across all indices. The VIX closed at 21.42, down from yesterday's close of 24.98. Of course, it's a long way back to 15 where I start to get comfortable. I suspect that might be a while. My T/A and P&F sums improved but are still well below 1. Money was coming into both the NYSE and NASDAQ early on but on a downtrend through the day to where it became negative from about 1:00 pm on. Today's action was not the beginning of an uptrend but a relief with a lot of buying from short covering. We need to see a big drop down and same day recovery before the next bottom is in place and I would like to see it next week with earnings announcements coming as downside surprises.

The S&P opened at 2771 (+43) and hit a high of 2776 (+48) before closing at 2767, up 39.

The Dow opened at 25408 (+355) and reached a high of 25468 (+415) and a midday low of 25001 (-52) before turning positive to close at 25340, up 287.

The Nas opened at 7508 (+179) and hit a high of 7517 (+188) before closing at 7497, up 168.

10/15/18

The market has resumed its old tricks of not providing direction. Choppy is the best description. The VIX hasn't eased up yet either closing at 21.23 and my T/A and P&F totals remain well below 1.

The S&P opened at 2764 (-3) and reached a high of 2776 (+9) and a low of 2749 late in the day and closed at 2751, down 16.

The Dow opened at 25332 (-8) and reached a high of 25482 (+142) and a low of 25244 (-96) before closing at 25251, down 89.

The Nas opened at 7473 (-24) and was briefly ahead at 7501 (+4) and a low of 7400 (-97) before closing at 7431, down 66.

Now that earnings announcements have begun it will be interesting to see how many stocks get punished or rewarded for their results.

10/16/18

The important question is was this a blow off or a recovery? All indices finished near the highs of the day and the VIX lost ground. The VIX closed at 17.64 down from yesterday's 21.23, and my T/A and P&F sums were above 1 for the first time since September 20.

The S&P opened at 2767 (+16) and achieved a high of 2813 (+62) before closing at 2810, up 59.

The Dow opened at 25352 (+101) and hit a high of 25818 (+567) before closing at 25798, up 548).

The Nas opened at 7502 (+71) and reached a high of 7658 (+227) before closing at 7645, up 215.

This was a very impressive and positive day and the fact that the indices closed near the intraday highs is certainly different from what we have been seeing for October. Let's hope that earnings come in without too many negative surprises.

10/17/18

Well, so much for two consecutive up days as all majors closed down. After a day like yesterday though it wasn't entirely unexpected. The VIX closed at 17.38 down from 17.62. The candle pattern was an inverted hammer. It could signal a change in direction which would mean that the VIX will go higher. My T/A and P&F sums were less than 1 as well.

The S&P opened at 2812 (+2) and reached a high of 2817 (+7) and a low of 2782 (-28) before closing at 2809, down 1. It remained above its 200 Day SMA and below its 50 Day SMA.

The Dow opened at 25706 (-92) and managed a high of 25810 (+12) and a low of 25479 (-319) before recovering somewhat to close at 25707, down 92. The Dow is above its 200 Day SMA but below its 50 Day SMA.

The Nas opened at 7669 (+24) and hit a high of 7670 (+25) and a low of 7563 (-82) before closing at 7643, down 3. Like the S&P and Dow, it is between its 200 and its 50 Day SMAs.

Basically, the market is in Limbo and will go up or down, in my opinion, in a big way before the week is out.

10/18/18

The choppiness has subsided! The market was in sell mode today and because tomorrow is a Friday, I expect a repeat and a correction of the stocks in the major indices. The VIX closed at 20.06, up 2.66 and my T/A and P&F sums ended below 1.

The S&P opened at 2802 (-7) and reached a low of 2755 (-54) and closed at 2769, down 40 points. It hung on to its 200 Day SMA by a thread.

The Dow opened at 25646 (-71) and hit a low of 25236 (-471) before closing at 25379, down 327. It is 222 points above its daily 200 Day SMA.

The Nas opened at 7616 (-27) and fell to an intraday low of 7452 (-191) before closing at 7485, down 158. It closed below its 200 Day SMA again.

Each of these indices are headed toward being oversold but aren't there yet. Maybe tomorrow.

10/19/18

The week pretty much ended without any clear resolution as to future direction. The VIX closed at 19.89 and is still well above its 50 and 200 Day SMAs and my T/A and P&F sums remained below 1. According to Tom Bowley of StockCharts.com.com, next week is the most bearish week statistically for the calendar year. It may be the period that determines market direction for the rest of the year. There are some who would like to see a retest of the February lows. A retest with a bounce afterwards would be bullish and help resolve any fears that traders might have held since the February/March timeframes.

The S&P opened at 2776 (+7) and reached an early high of 2798 (+29) before fading for the rest of the day with a low of 2760 (-9). The index closed at 2768, down 1.

The Dow opened at 25421 (+42) and reached an intraday high of 25609 (+230) and a low of 25350 (-29) before closing at 25444, up 65.

The Nas opened at a promising 7530 (+45) and hit 7583 (+98) early before losing ground to hit an intraday low of 7428 (-57) before closing at 7449, down 36. It closed down 8.4% from its all-time high of 8133. The S&P is down 6.2% and the Dow is 5.6% from the respective highs of just a few weeks ago.

10/22/18

And the river that is the market lately, choppy with a bit of a drop! Although slightly lower the VIX closed at 19.57 and remains well above its simple moving averages (SMAs). Needless to say, my T/A and P&F sums is in the doldrums at .3% favorable. The Nas managed to close in the green. The Russell 2000 also showed promise but couldn't close favorably. The Nas is 8.1% off its high and the Russell is 11.6% down. The Nas was down 10% on October 11. Some improvement there. This means both of these indices have been in correction territory at one time or another. Time will tell when the Dow and S&P follow suit.

The S&P opened at 2774 (+6) and hit a high of 2779 (+11) and a low of 2749 (-19), closing at 2756, down 12.

The Dow opened at 25492 (+48) and reached a high of 25561 (+117) early and then trailed off to 25236

(-208) finally closing at 25317, down 127.

The Nas opened at 7487 (+38) and hit a low of 7425 (-24) before climbing to 7521 (+72). It couldn't keep that support and closed at 7469, up 20.

10/23/18

I began keeping the T/A and P&F sums in March 2016 and the lowest percentage I had was on February 5, 2018, when it was 10.9%. Today it was 14.8%. I'm betting that it will eventually hit that mark again and that could mark a bottom. Or Not! I'm afraid it may go lower. Today it means that securities showing up in the bullish patterns were 14.8% of the total of the four columns. Today that total was 1674 bullish and 9618 bearish for a total of 11292. It may happen that an equity may show up in a couple of patterns on the same day and skew the numbers, but I suspect that there would be offsets. The VIX closed at 20.94 and had been as high as 24.66. I suspect we will see it go higher sometime soon.

The S&P opened at 2721 (-35) and hit a low of 2691 (-65) in the first hour of trade. It did recover throughout the day and close at 2741, down 15.

The Dow opened at 25038 (-279) eventually hitting a low of 24769 (-548) before closing at 25191, down 126.

The Nas opened at 7329 (-140) and hit a low of 7260 (-209) and a high of 7473 (+4) and closed at 7438, down 31.

All of the indices experienced buying in the late afternoon, but the damage had been done with the morning lows. Until the indices find support at some credible level the overall direction will be geared toward that goal. I'm not optimistic.

The S&P was down 8.5% at its low today from its all-time high. The Dow was down 8.1% from its all-time high and the Nas was down 10.7 from its all-time high. Should the S&P and Dow follow suit it would mean a further decline of 2.2 % for the S&P, 65 more points and for the Dow 2.6% or another 701 points. Although I rarely reference the Russell 2000 it bears looking at now as an indicator of what could possibly happen in terms of a correction. Today's low was 1501. That's 13.8% off its all-time high.

10/24/18

What an end to the day! Every index had a dead weight attached and they sank bigtime, all within the last 45 minutes. The S&P closed at 2656, down 85 points (3.09%). The Dow closed at 24583, down 608

(2.41%) and the Nas closed at 7108, down 329 (4.43%). The VIX closed at 26.32, up 5.61 from yesterday. Its high was 26.38. Will it push to 50 before week's end? Stay tuned.

The S&P opened at 2738 (-3) and managed a high of 2743 (+2) before going downhill and eventually touching a low of 2652 (-89) before closing at 2656 and 9.7% off its all-time high.

The Dow opened at 25172 (-18) and started well, hitting a high of 25306 (+115) before its fall to 24533

(-658) and closed at 24583. It closed 8.8% off its all-time high.

The Nas opened at 7423 (-15) and slid to an intraday low of 7099 (-339) before closing at 7108. It closed down 12.6% from its all-time high.

The Russell and Nas are both in correction territory using 10% as the lower limit. The S&P and Dow still have a way to go to join the group. My concern is that we are looking at around 15%.

10/25/18

Today was a bounce day. It looked good when reviewing the indices but there was nothing to indicate that bottoms were put in place yesterday. With the decent increases today, I would have expected to see at least some improvement in the bull side of my sums, but those numbers were lower. In fact, the P&F bear sum grew. The T/A bear sum dropped considerably which could indicate that the Russell and Nasdaq, both of which are in correction, may be leveling off. The VIX fell to 24.10, down 1.13. That is still a dangerously high value and it is best to keep to the sidelines unless you can trade without losing sight of where your stock is heading in the next two minutes or have appropriate stops in place. There was no dramatic sell-off (sales on high volume) or heavy volume on the moves up today.

The S&P opened at 2675 (+19) and reached an afternoon high of 2723 (+67) before closing at 2706, up 49 or 1.9%.

The Dow opened at 24737 (+154) and hit 25104 (+521) late in the afternoon, closing at 24985, up 401 or 1.6%.

The Nas opened at 7197 (+89) and rose to a high of 7365 (+257) before closing at 7318, up 210 or 3%. This brings it back to 10% off its high of 8133, still correction territory.

The Russell closed at 1500 after rising 2.2%. It remains 13.9% off its high.

10/26/18

There are some in the StockCharts.com group who believe we may be entering a bear market rather than a period of correction because of so many broken charts of indices and equities/ETFs. I can only offer that I have more and more confidence in my T/A and P&F sum results to say that I'm leaning toward a 15 – 20% correction based on the big hits that so many stocks have taken. As we go forward, I would expect to see a continuation of trading similar to this week, with the general direction ending down. The VIX is screaming RISKY, so if you are trading don't leave your platform because of the potential quick sentiment change that is likely. It closed at 24.16.

This was not a fun week and it doesn't look like things will change with the exception of one or two possible up days per week at best.

The S&P opened at 2668 (-38) and managed a low of 2628 (-78) before recovering to 2659, down 47.

The Dow opened at 24770 (-215) and hit a low of 24445 (-540) and closed at 24688, down 296.

The Nas opened at 7125 (-193) and dropped to a low of 7057 (-261) closing at 7167, down 151.

The S&P closed 9.6% below its all-time high and at its low of 2628 was 11.9% off the high. This index opened the year at 2674 and closed today 15 points below the start of the year.

The Dow closed 8.4 % off its all-time high and at its low of 24445 was 9.3% below its all-time high. It remains the only major index above a 10% correction level. It is 31 points below its start for the year.

The Nas closed 11.9% below its all-time high and at its low today was 13.2% below it. It is 264 points ahead for the year.

An intraday 15% correction for the Nas and possibly S&P seems very possible next week. Hitting that might stimulate some buying of stocks associated with them.

10/29/18

It started off to be positive across the board but ended the day in its usual fashion of late. BA was down today as well because of a LION flight that went down and that might have had added some negative bias. It was a newly built 737-800.

The VIX did close higher at 24.73 after being as low as 22.01 this morning and a high of 27.86. This created a negative box fill on my daily P&F chart that I keep. Although it's too early to make a determination, MY T/A and P&F closed at .40 which is the highest that it has been since 10/17. So, some equities are on the move…at least they were today.

The S&P opened at 2683 (+24) and hit a high of 2707 (+48) early in the session and a low of 2604 (-55) before closing at 2641, down 17.

The Dow opened at 24819 (+131) and managed a high of 25041(+353) and a low of 24122 (-566) before closing at 24443, down 245.

The Nas opened at 7272 (+105) and stretched it to an early high of 7296 (+129) before reversing to hit a low of 6923 (-244) and closed at 7050, down 117. The Nas did bounce off of a support line that I placed a while back.

The Dow and S&P have been bouncing off of its lower Bollinger band and in the past, this has signaled the end of a downtrend and a rally. Every index is also showing oversold or soon to be RSIs of +/- 30. So, I am looking for some rallying although it might be brief.

10/30/18

And today was choppy but ended nicely for a change! The indices closed near the highs of the day as well. As you would expect the VIX dropped to 23.41 from yesterday's 24.73. Still too high but moving in the right direction. My T/A and P&F sums also moved higher to a ratio of .58 and it was nice to see all of the green bars on the bull side for a change. I don't have any great expectations because tomorrow could be a return to the nastiness. But I'm guessing that we should have at least one more positive day because of the closes being near the day's highs. All indices turned from the 30 RSI, but just barely. So, the conditions are still good for at least one more positive day.

The S&P opened at yesterday's close of 2641 and hit an early low of 2635 (-6). Choppy all day, it finally took off to a high of 2685 (+44) and closed at 2683, up 41.

The Dow opened at 24482 (+39) and managed a low early of 24416 (-27) and struggled for most of the day before reaching its intraday high of 24907 (+464) prior to its close of 24875, up 432.

The Nas opened at 7018 (-32) reaching a low of 7001 (-49) and chopped to a high of 7167 (+117) and closed at 7162, up 111.

10/31/18

Today was the last day of October and I'm pretty sure most traders are happy to see it in their review mirror. It ended on a good note but closed well off their highs for the day. The VIX closed at 21.06, down 2.29. The PPO dropped a tad below the signal line and that's promising. My T/A and P&F bull pattern equities both improved very nicely, and the bear sums dropped. The sums closed above 1 for

the first time since October 16. It has closed above 1 only three times in the last 30 trading days and four times in the last 48 trading days.

The S&P started the month at 2913 and closed it at 2712 for a loss of 201 points or 6.9%. At its low for the month the index was down 11.9% intraday.

The Dow began October at 26458 and closed at 25116 for a loss of 1342 or 5.1%. Its monthly intraday low saw a 9.3% loss.

The NAS suffered the worst with a start of 8046 and a close today of 7306. That's am monthly loss of 9.2%. At its low for the month it was off 13.2%.

These indices had a tough month to say the least but there are no assurances that it's onward and upward from here. It's much harder going up a muddied hill than it is sliding down one.

The S&P opened at 2706 (+23) and reached a high of 2737 (+54) and closed at 2712, up 29.

The Dow opened at 25009 (+134) and hit a high of 25337 (+462) intraday, closing at 25116, up 241.

The Nas opened at 7277 (+115) and reached 7368 (+206) intraday, closing at 7306, up 144.

November

11/01/18

Today marked the third day of nice performances across the indices. They also closed near their highs for the day with lows of the day coming early on. The VIX closed at 19.34, down 1.89. It is still too high to make me comfortable, so we need to keep an eye out. My T/A and P&F sums ended at 1.8 (yeah)! That's two days over 1 in a row and that hasn't happened since September13-14. Unless technicals continue to improve for the major indices this needs to be viewed as a relief rally and short-lived. With the current feeling that the democrats will just take back the house, traders are looking at two years of gridlock. That may explain why this rally has begun.

The Nas remains well below its 200 Day SMA although the PPO has merged with the signal line but is at a negative 2. The Dow did cross above its 200 Day SMA with room to spare and its PPO merged with its signal line as well. It is slightly below -1. The S&P and Russell 2000 closed below their 200 Day SMAs, but the PPO merged with its respective signal lines as well. Even though the charts remain busted they are on their way to the repair shop.

The S&P opened at 2718 (+6) and chopped to a morning low of 2709 (-3) and then evened out to climb to a high of 2742 (+30) before closing at 2740, up 29.

The Dow opened at 25142 (+26) and hit a low of 25108 (-8) before gaining altitude and reaching a high of 25396 (+280) and closing at 25381, up 265.

The Nas opened at 7328 (+2) and slid to a low of 7286 (-20) before regaining its footing to close at 7434, up 128.

11/02/18

It was time for profit taking as only the Russell finished the day in the green. All indices were up initially because of a news report that a trade deal with China was being hammered out. A correction was made later inferring that there was no deal in the works at which time the market started heading lower. The VIX moved higher initially as the selling began building energy but ended the day at 19.44 at a slight gain. My T/A and P&F sums ended well above 1 for the third day in a row. I sold everything when the indices started south and only left GLD on the table. I would have done so at day's end anyway because I didn't want to be long over the weekend, especially this one because of the mid-term elections coming Tuesday and because all indices charts are broken. Apparently, many traders felt the same as me.

The S&P opened at 2745 (+5) and reached an early high of 2757 (+17) before dropping as low as 2700

(-40) midday. It closed at 2726, down 17.

The Dow opened at 25444 (+63) and almost immediately hit its high of 25579 (+198) and a low of 25079 (-302) before rising to close at 25271, down 110.

The Nas opened at 7424 (-12) and did hit a high of 7467 (+110) early on but then headed south to settle on a low of 7299 (-135) before recovering somewhat to close at 7357, down 77.

All in all, it was a good week with the S&P gaining 64, The Dow gaining 583 and the Nas gaining 190 since last Friday's close.

11/05/18

It was a good day with the &P and Dow up pretty decently and the Nas was down slightly. The VIX rose to 19.91, up .40 and my T/A and P&F sums closed over 1 again. I'm getting a little comfortable about the immediate future of the market in that there shouldn't be much in the way of any great correction but remain cautious until the technicals improve.

The S&P opened at 2726 (+3) and hit a low of 2718 (-5) and a high of 2744 (+21) before closing at 2738, up 15.

The Dow opened at 25261 (-10) and reached a high of 25507 (+236) before closing at 25462, up 191.

The Nas opened at 7344 (-13) and dropped to a low of 7256 (-101) and recovered most of the loss to close at 7329, down 28.

11/06/18

The long-awaited Election Day! The markets did well, and the majors all closed up. Now we await the results and pre-markets to see what the changes will bring. The VIX closed slightly down at 19.85 and my T/A and P&F remained above 1. Perhaps we are temporarily out of the woods. The Dow is still below its 50 Day SMA and the other indices are moving toward their 200 Day SMAs. It would be telling to see them close above them this week.

The S&P opened at 2738, yesterday's close and hit an afternoon low of 2737 (-1) but was up most of the day. After hitting a high of 2757 (+19) near the close it backed off slightly to close at 2755, up 17.

The Dow opened at 25453 (-9) and chopped, eventually hitting a low of 25445 (-17) and closed at 25635, up 173, which was just slightly off its late in the day high of 25652 (+190).

The Nas opened at 7326 (-3) and reached a low of 7321 (-8) and intraday high of 7401 (+72) before closing its choppy session at 7376, up 47.

11/07/18

Today's market activity validated the comfort that traders feel because congressional gridlock is pretty much guaranteed, and the mid-term fears resolved favorably. The House majority is democrat and the Senate republican. Today's activity went a long way in fixing the technical damage inflicted in October. The Dow closed above its 50 Day SMA and the S&P and Nas closed above their 200 Day SMAs. Perhaps they can close above their 50 Day SMAs this week as well. At any rate the bulls were very much in charge. My T/A and P&F were well over 1 and above 1 for six days running now.

The S&P opened at 2774 (+19) and hit a high of 2815 (+60) toward day's end and closing at 2814, up 58.

The Dow opened at 25788(+153) and hit a high of 26200 (+565) and closed at 26180, up 545.

The Nas opened at 7446 (+70) and hit 7573 near the close before actually closing at 7571, up 195, 2.64%. Both the S&P and Dow closed over 2.1% as well. Pretty significant!

11/08/18

The indices were down with the exception of the Dow as profit taking ensued after yesterday's nice gains. I believe it was important that the Nas and S&P remained above their 200 Day SMAs and the Dow remained above its 50 Day SMA as well. The VIX closed at 16.73 after an intraday high of 17.20. My T/A and P&F sums remained above 1 and the bull P&F was higher than yesterday while the bear was lower than yesterday. I believe that the P&F sums carry more weight because movement is much slower due to the nature of P&F charting. I am now almost 88% invested because of the confidence that I'm gaining from my T/A and P&F sums data base.

The S&P opened at 2806 (-8) and hit a mid-day high of 2815 (+1) and a low of 2795 (-19) but recovered somewhat to close at 2807, up 7.

The Dow opened at 26140 (-40) and ranged between a low of 26082 (-98) and a high of 26278 (+98) and barely managed a positive close at 26191, up 11.

The Nas opened at 7544 (-27) and managed an intraday low of 7500 (-71) before recovering to close at 7531, down 40.

11/09/18

The indices all closed down today but well off of their lows. The S&P flirted with its 200 Day SMA but closed above it. The Dow touched its 50 Day SMA but finished the session above it. These tests were not unexpected, and it was good to see them resolve favorably. The Nas on the other hand closed below its 200 Day SMA. The VIX closed up .68 to 17.40. It was as high as 18.41 intraday, so I view this in a favorable light. My T/A and P&F sums closed below 1 for the first time in eight days. I will remain positive as long as this pattern doesn't last for too long.

The S&P opened at 2794 (-13) and reached a low of 2764 (-43) and recovered some to close at 2781, down 26. It is up 58 for the week.

The Dow opened at 26149 (-42) and managed a low of 25883 (-308) but scrambled back to close at 25989, down 202. For the week it gained 718.

The Nas opened at 7469 (-62) and hit an intraday low of 7349 (-182) but regained some to close at 7407, down 124. It gained 50 for the week.

Though I could end up eating these words next week, I expect it to be a positive one based upon the technicals that I see in reviewing today's results. Time will tell.

11/12/18

Tomorrow I will go to nearly all cash again at the earliest opportunity! Today was not a good day across all indices. I thought we had cleared some nice hurdles when the S&P and Nas closed above their 200 Day SMAs last week, but it didn't last, and the Dow dropped below its 50. There just doesn't appear to be any buying momentum and too much eagerness to sell after any day or string of days that were positive.

The VIX closed at 20.45 after a golden cross completed its pattern last Monday, November 5. At that point traders were waiting for the election outcome so my concern was minor, and it kept closing lower until last Thursday. Technically, we should be seeing higher closes in the future because the crossover is bullish. My T/A and P&F sums closed below 1 again.

The Dow closed down 602 points, the S&P was down 55 points and the Nas closed down 206 points! Not a fun day at all, particularly if you weren't watching the markets.

The S&P opened at 2774 (-7) and headed down all day with a low of 2722 (-59) and closed at 2726, down 55.

The Dow opened at 25959 (-30) reaching its low of 25341 (-648) before closing at 25387, down 602.

The Nas opened at 7364 (-43) before hitting its intraday low of 7194 (-213) and closed at 7201, down 206.

11/13/18

Today started and ended the way it has so many times this year. The morning starts out to be promising but ends down or no change. The VIX did close down slightly at 20.02 after leveling off from a high of 21.25. A look at its chart indicates a move higher. My T/A and P&F sums were lower as well with no indication of seeing better results anytime soon. And to make matters worse it appears that the Russell 2K is going to complete a death cross. That is where the shorter duration average (50 Day SMA) crosses below the longer duration average (200 Day SMA. If not corrected immediately it implies that greater pain is coming.

The S&P opened at 2730 (+4) and hit a high of 2755 (+29) and a low of 2715 (-11) before closing at 2722, down 4.

The Dow opened at 25321 (-66) and reached a high of 25511 (+124) and a low of 25194 (-193) before closing at 25286, down 101.

The Nas opened at 7231 (+30) and hit a high of 7319 (+118) and a low of 7183 (-18) before closing at 7201, yesterday's close as well.

11/14/18

Same thing different day! The day started off positively enough, but the short rally ended like the others from the past seven weeks or so, in negative territory. Today saw a decent rise in the VIX to 21.26 a T/A and P&F sums remaining well below 1 and the Dow below its 200 Day SMA. So, all major indices are below their 200 Day SMAs. The Russell 2K isn't quite there yet with completing its death cross but tomorrow should do it.

No talking heads om CNBC or the StockCharts.com crew is looking for any sustaining rally because the technicals don't support one. Some indices are looking like inverse H&S patterns are forming but it is doubtful that these will be completed.

The S&P opened at 2738 (+16) and climbed to a high of 2747 (+25) before drifting to a low of 2686 (-36) before closing at 2702, down 21.

The Dow opened in a promising manner as well at 25388 (+102) but skidded to a low of 24936 (-350) before recovering to close at 25080, down 206.

The Nas opened at with the most promise at 7265 (+ 64) and hit a high of 7286 (+85) but inched down to a low of 7101 (-100) before closing at 7136, down 64.

Maybe we'll rally tomorrow and keep it. But I'm not expecting anything even if it comes to fruition because there is no promise from the technical side.

11/15/18

Judging from the indices closes it appeared to be a good rally day. But underneath it all there is nothing to see that would lead me to believe that this was nothing more than a run of the mill relief rally.

The VIX closed at 20.02 down 1.19 from yesterday and my T/A and P&F sums moved slightly higher in total, but the bull P&F sums were lower, and the bear P&F sums were higher. That's a problem! There were no improvements regarding changes in the indices with regard to any moving averages. The other bad news is that the Russell 2K completed its death cross today.

The S&P opened at 2694 (-8) and dropped to 2671 (-31) and moved up to a high of 2735 (+33) before closing at 2730, up 29.

The Dow opened at 25061 (-19) and hit a low of 24788 (-292) before moving as high as 25355 (+275) before closing at 25289, up 209.

The Nas opened at 7113 (-23) and hit a low of 7072 (-64) and an intraday high of 7274 (+138) and closed at 7259, up 123.

11/16/18

The S&P and Dow closed up and the Nas closed lower. The VIX dropped to 18.14, lower by 1.84 and there was improvement with my T/A and P&F sums. However, the VIX remained well above its moving averages and my sums are below 1. The is a possibility that the SPY has formed a H&S pattern which would be a positive move. We'll see if it completes next week. I have done some day-trading but closed to cash at the end of the day except for USO and TWTR.

The S&P opened at 2719 (-11) and dropped to 2712 (-18) before chopping to a high of 2747 (+17) prior to closing at 2736, up 6.

The Dow opened at 25242 (-47) and hit a low of 25148 (-241) and a high of 25510 (+221) before closing at 25413, up 124.

The Nas opened at 7194 (-65) and reached a low of 7172 (-87) and a high of 7275 (+16) and then closed at 7248, down 11.

11/19/18

Well, another sucky Monday! The indices were all down more than 1.5% with the Nas being the biggest loser at 3.03%. The VIX was up 2 closing at 20.14 and my T/A and P&F sums ended at .44. The Nas is now just days away from forming its death cross and the Dow has joined the others in closing below its 200 Day SMA.

The S&P opened at 2731 (-5) and hit a low of 2681 (-55), closing with little improvement at 2691, down 46.

The Dow opened at 25393 (-20) and slid to a low of 24901 (-512) before closing at 25017, down 396.

The Nas opened at 7217 (-31) and drifted to a low of 7011 (-237) before closing at 7028, down 219.

I'm hoping that the Nas low is in place after matching its October low and the DOW and S&P have formed inverse H&S patterns indicating that lows are now in place. It's the best that can be hoped for now given the technical indicators.

11/20/18

Today was another awful day for traders unless you were shorting. The indices were all down around 2% with the Dow higher than 2% while the others were down less than 2%. The VIX was a winner closing at 22.56 and my T/A and S&P sums closed at .18. We could see a relief rally I suppose but I wouldn't count on it too heavily. The safest bet is day trading with a careful eye throughout the day. Of the three major indices only the Nas is higher than the start of the year and that's by just 6 points. So, not a pretty scenario being painted here.

The S&P opened at 2655 (-36) and hit a low of 2632 (-59) before closing at 2642, down 49. It closed last year at 2673 and is negative for the year by 31 points.

The Dow opened at 24619 (-398) and reached a low of 24369 (-648) before closing at 24466, down 552. It ended last year at 24719. It is down 253 points YTD.

The Nas opened at 6867 (-161) and hit a low of 6831 (-197) before closing at 6909, down 120. It began the year at 6903.

Thinking back, we have been here done that at least twice before during this calendar year.

11/21/18

There was a rally of sorts today, but it fizzled as the day progressed. The VIX dropped to 20.80 but still remains in a favorable position of moving higher with higher lows and higher highs for the last two weeks. It gapped down twice and has one more to fill in. My T/A and P&F sums remain below 1 although improved somewhat. Friday is an abbreviated session and will likely be up at the close. We'll see.

The S&P opened at 2658 (+16) and reached a high of 2671 (+29) but couldn't sustain most of the increase and closed at 2650, up 8.

The Dow opened at 24542 (+76) and hit a high of 24670 (+204) that it couldn't sustain and closed at 24465, down 1.

The Nas opened at 6986 (+77) and jumped to 7030 (+121) before closing at 6975, up 63.

It is likely that today's highs were achieved by traders closing their short positions prior to taking the next four days off.

11/23/18

Today was a very lackluster trading day. It was also Black Friday. Not much to report on because the markets are in a boring slump. The VIX rose again and is now at 21.52. Nothing in the way of interest either regarding my T/A and P&F sums. The Nas is the only index that is favorable for the year by a margin of 36 points.

The S&P opened at 2633 (-17) and hit its low of 2631 (-19) before closing at 2633, down 17. It is down 103 for the week.

The Dow opened at 24366 (-129) and reached a low of 24269 (-196) before closing at 24286, down 179. It lost 1127 points this week.

The Nas opened at 6920 (-52) and slid to a low of 6919 (-53) and closed at 6939, down 33. It lost 309 points this week.

Next week will be a full trading week with all hands-on deck. The three RSIs are at 33-35 which is still above oversold therefore I don't believe we will see much, if any, relief rally.

11/26/18

Today was a more positive day than we have been seeing and possibly showed promise that we could have a relief rally as we move closer to Christmas. The VIX remains high closing at 18.90 but dropped from Friday's 21.52 and my T/A and P&F sums ended the day below 1.

The S&P opened at 2650 (+17) and hit a high of 2674 (+41) before closing at 2673, up 40.

The Dow opened at 24364 (+78) and reached its high of 24673 (+387) before closing at 24640, up 354.

The Nas opened at 7026 (+87) and hit a high of 7084 (+145) before closing at 7082, up 143.

Hopefully, we will see a few more days like this in the future.

11/27/18

Today was another positive day, so, two out of two for the week. There was nothing special in the news. The VIX closed at 19.02. That is up from yesterday's 18.90. My T/a and P&F sums still show nothing positive either.

The S&P opened at 2664 (-9) and hit a low of 2656 (-17) and a high of 2683 (+10) before closing at 2682, up 9.

The Dow opened at 24557 (-83) and reached a low of 24416 (-224) and a high of 24751 (+111) before closing at 24749, up 109.

The Nas opened at 7041 (-41) and hit its low of 7014 (-68) and its high of 7105 (+23) and closed at 7083, up 1.

11/28/18

Today was a rare day, but in the best way. The indices were higher at the open and it looked like another positive one like the last two days. Then Fed Chair, Jay Powell, spoke at around noon, indicating for the first time during his tenure that rates are getting close to "neutral". The bulls heard all that was needed. The markets took off, big time! Volumes were up across all of the indices but not alarmingly so and it was one of the best closes this year. The indices close were near the highs for the day. Additionally, many world markets joined in the rally.

The VIX improved somewhat, closing at 18.49. That's the lowest close since November 16 but still too high to ignore. My T/A and P&F sums closed above 1 for the first time since November 8. Hard to tell what tomorrow will bring but the first three days of this week have been very welcome.

The S&P opened at 2691 (+9) and reached an intraday and closing high of 2744, up 62.

The Dow opened at 24833 (+84) and climbed to a high of 25369 (+620) before closing at 25366, up 617.

The Nas opened at 7135 (+52) and hit a high of 7293 (+210) before closing at 7292, up 209.

And the Russell closed up 37. This indicates participation of the small caps as well.

11/29/18

Today the indices were all down at the close but after yesterday's performance it was not unexpected. There was profit taking as traders took what they could after Powell's gift to them. The VIX remained high at 18.72 and its chart is still healthy with a close above its 50 Day SMA. My T/A and P&F sums remained above 1. That's two days in a row. The charts of the major indices are improving, and the current correction seems to have bottomed. But they are still broken and the best that can be hoped for is a seasonal rally or some positive trading outcome during the G20 summit this weekend. We'll see.

The S&P opened at 2737 (-7) and hit a low of 2723 (-21) and a high of 2754 (+10) before closing at 2738, down 6.

The Dow opened at 25344 (-22) and registered a low of 25203 (-163) and a high of 25479 (+113) before closing at 25339, down 27.

The Nas opened at 7267 (-25) and reached a low of 7218 (-74) and a high of 7320 (+28) before closing at 7273, down 19.

11/30/18

Today was the last day of November and the indices closed higher. Every day ended higher with Thursday being the exception. The VIX closed at 18.07 and ended below its 50 Day SMA for the first time since November 9. It remains well above the 15 comfort zone. My T/A and P&F sums were over 1 for

The third day in a row.

Unfortunately, the Dow remained below its 50 Day SMA and the S&P below its 200 Day SMA. The Nas has not modified the direction of its 50 Day SMA, so its death cross, formed on Monday, remains in place with the Russell 2K.

The S&P opened at 2738 (prior close) and hit a low of 2733 (-5) and a high of 2761 (+23) before closing at 2760, up 22.

The Dow opened at 25308 (-32) and reached a low of 25251 (-88) and a high of 25550 (+211) before closing at 25538, up 200.

The Nas opened at 7279 (+6) and hit a low of 7256 (-17) and a high of 7333 (+60) before closing at 7331, up 57.

The S&P is up 87 points for the year, the Dow 919 points and the Nas 464. YTD – Nothing to write home about. Maybe December will improve our fortunes.

December

12/03/18

President George H.W. Bush died Friday night. The markets will be closed on Wednesday, December 5 in his honor.

With the pre-market jumps you would have thought that the U.S. and China had finalized a deal. In the end though, nothing was really different. The president simply put off the next round of tariff increases for 90 days.

The VIX closed at 16.36 and remained above its 200 Day SMA. Perhaps that will change tomorrow. My T/A and P&F sums closed well above 1. But there was a promising event this morning that did not pan out by day's end. The Nas gapped above its 50 Day SMA early but closed below it at the market close. Perhaps it will close above the 50 Day SMA tomorrow, but I don't think that's a given. On the bright side though, the Russell 2K closed above its 50 Day SMA and the Dow and S&P closed above its 50 Day SMA. The Nas and Russell inverse SMAs have not changed.

The S&P opened at 2790 (+30) and hit a high of 2800 (+40) in early trading before closing at 2790, up 30.

The Dow opened at 25780 (+242) and reached a high of 25980 before losing steam to close at 25826, up 288.

The Nas opened at 7486 (+155) and achieved its high of 7487 (+156) before closing at 7442, up 111.

12/04/18

Today threw me totally off-guard. I believed that if the markets were going to have a down day it would have Monday, not today. For longs it was another terrible day. I bought in the morning hours when I should have stayed out. The Dow was down over 800 points and the other indices were just as devastated.

To my surprise the VIX did rise during the day but not in a telling manner. It closed at 20.74, up 4.30, and only reached a high of 21.94 before settling down. Right or wrong, this action tells me that trades were handled for the most part without the usual fear that we have in the past with such big market drops. My T/A and P&F sums ended well below 1 for the first time in five days.

The S&P opened at 2782 (-8) and spent the morning in a minor downtrend. And then at noon the real slide began and followed through for the rest of the session hitting a low of 2697 (-93) before closing 2700, down 90.

The Dow opened at 25753 (-73) and patterned the S&P throughout the day. It achieved a low of 25008 (-818) before closing at 25027, down 799.

The Nas opened at 7408 (-34) and reached a low of 7150 (-292) before it closed at 7158, down 284.

The Dow and S&P were down 3.24% and 3.1% respectively while the bigger hits were taken by the Nas down by 3.7% and the Russell 2K 4.4%.

12/06/18

The pomp and circumstances involved with Bush 41's funeral yesterday was absolutely inspiring. Both sides of the aisle were as one voice as the nation honored a great man. When reasons and events arise to give Americans an opportunity to put aside differences, even for just one day, you realize what a great country we have and that it needs to be preserved for future generations. Thank you, George H.W. Bush, for your leadership and moral example and your many years of service.

Now to the market.

The S&P opened at 2664 (-36) and reached a low of 2622 (-78) before closing at 2696, down 4. Volume was high at 5.1 million shares.

The Dow opened at 24737 (-290) and hit its low of 24242 (-785) before recovering to close at 24948, down 79.

The Nas opened at 7017 (-141) and hit a low of 6984 (-174) before closing at 7188, up 30 and just slightly off its high of 7190 (+32).

The VIX closed at 21.19 and my T/A and P&F sums closed below 1. I liked the way the indices closed after having been down most of the day. Perhaps we'll see a relief rally beginning tomorrow.

12/07/18

What a bummer of a week, man! We lost 4.6% of our portfolio. I can't imagine what it was like for anyone having to cover margin calls or selling stocks not margined to help cover the calls.

The Dow started the week at 25538 and ended it at 24389, down 1149 points and 4.5%. The S&P began at 2760 and ended the week at 2633, down 127 points and 4.6%. The Nas opened the week at 7331 and closed out the week at 6969, down 362 points and 4.9%.

The S&P is now down 308 points from its 2018 high of 2941 or 10.5%. The Dow is down 2563 points from its high and 9.5%. The Nas is off 1164 points from its high this year and 14.3%.

The S&P opened at 2691 (-5) and managed a high of 2709 (+13) before dropping to 2623 (-73) before edging up to 2633, down 63.

The Dow opened at 24919 (-29) and reached a high of 25096 (+148) before its slide to a low of 24285 (-663) before closing at 24389, down 559.

The Nas opened at 7163 (-25) and still mustered a high of 7205 (+17) before closing in on its low of 6945 (-243) and ended at 6969, down 219.

YTD the S&P is off 41 points, the Dow 330 points and the Nas is up 66 points.

12/10/18

This was an interesting day. The indices all looked determined to make new lows but pulled up mid- way through the day to put in some pretty good highs, only to close a few points above Friday's close. The VIX closed at 22.64 and my T/A and P&F sums ended at .189, one of the lowest values of the year.

The S&P opened at 2631 (-2) and reached a low of 2583 (-50) and a high of 2648 (-15) before closing at 2638, up 5.

The Dow opened at 24361 (-28) and hit an intraday low of 23881 (-508) and a high of 24501 (+112) prior to closing at 24423, up 34.

The Nas opened at 6960 (-9) and reached its low of 6879 (-90) and a high of 7048 (-79) before closing at 7021, up 52.

12/11/18

We see this pattern of the trading day repeated often now. The indices open higher and hit an early high only to see the buying reverse with the index down for the fay or closing up but well off of the highs for the day. The indices are rangebound since October and all indications are that we are in a bear market or soon will be. But we remain hopeful that we will see a move to the old highs in anticipation of a Santa Claus rally. Time will tell of course, but my optimism has faded.

The VIX closed at 21.84. That's slightly higher than yesterday and exceedingly high. My T/A and P&F improved slightly to 33.7.

The S&P opened at 2664 (+26) and reached a high of 2674 (+36) and a low of 2621 (-17) before recovering enough to close at 2637, down 1.

The Dow performed much the same way opening at 24720 (+297) and hit a high of 24791 (+368) and a low of 24221 (-202) before reversing course to close at 24370, down 53.

The Nas opened at 7122 (+101) and reached a high of 7130 (+109) and a low of 6983 (-38) and recovered some to close at 7032, up 11.

12/12/18

The indices opened higher and continued higher throughout the day before losing steam and giving up most of the day's gains by the market's close. The VIX closed lower than Tuesday's close at 21.46. Needless to say, my T/A and P&F sums remain below 1. There is no question that we are at best in a correction and most likely in the early stages of a bear market. Cash should now be your best bet.

The S&P opened at 2658 (+21) and reached a high of 2685 (+48) before losing ground to close at 2651, up 14.

The Dow opened at 24509 (+139) and hit a high of 24828 (+458) before closing at 24527, up 157.

The Nas opened at 7127 (+95) and reached a high of 7197 (+165) before closing at 7098, up 66.

12/13/18

Another day of the market second guessing itself. It started up in the morning to gradually slip and turned somewhat in the final hour. Needless to say, the VIX remained above 20 at 20.65 and down fractionally from Wednesday.

The S&P opened at 2659 (+8) and hit a high of 2670 (+19) and a low of 2637 (-14) before closing at 2651, yesterday's close as well.

The Dow opened at 24576 (+49) and reached a high of 24741 (+214) and a low of 24473 (-54) before closing at 24597, up 70.

The Nas opened at 7135 (+37) and reached a high of 7155 (+57) and a low of 7035 (-63) before closing at 7070, down 28.

12/14/18

This day should have come as no surprise given the previous four days performance. The indices all opened down and remained negative for the rest of the day. Rallies, if any will be short-lived and I expect that Santa Clause is going to skip Wall Street this time. The VIX closed at 21.79 so no good news there. The Grinch continues lurking in the shadows.

The S&P opened at 2630 (-21) and reached a low of 2594 (-57) before closing at 2600, down 51.

The Dow opened at 24408 (-189) and hit a low of 24034 (-563) before closing at 24101, down 497.

The Nas opened at 6986 (-84) and reached a low of 6899 (-171) before closing at 6911, down 160.

12/17/18

More bloodshed today. But a relief rally shouldn't be too far off according to the RSIs of the major indices. The VIX closed at 24.56 and my T/A and P&F have reached previous low closing at .161. "His heart was two sizes too small". From "How the Grinch Stole Christmas!

The S&P opened at 2591 (-9) and hit a low of 2531 (-69) before closing at 2546, down 54.

The Dow opened at 23987, (-114) and reached a low of 23457 (-644) before closing at 23593, down 508.

The Nas opened at 6886 (-25) and hit a low of 6710 (-201) prior to closing at 6754, down 157.

12/18/18

It was a whipsaw day with indices highs occurring early on and the lows coming late in the day with some recovery from the lows. (Heard this before?) The VIX closed at 25.69, up 1.17 and the NYSE and NASDAQ continue bleeding cash throughout most of the day. "You're a foul one, Mr. Grinch". From "How the Grinch Stole Christmas!"

The S&P opened at 2560 (+14) and reached a high of 2574 (+28) and a low of 2529 (-17) before closing at 2546, yesterday's close.

The Dow opened at 23769 (+176) and hit a high of 23928 (+335) and later allow of 23516 (-77) before closing at 23676, up 83.

The Nas opened at 6886 (+132) its high for the day and reached a low of 6734 (-20) before closing at 6784, up 30.

There is a possibility of a Santa rally, but it will be from lows not yet seen, and these past weeks cold be a correction rather than the start of a bear market. I'm leaning toward the bear.

12/19/18

Fed Chair Powell spoke, and the markets didn't want to hear about two more rate hikes in 2019. My belief is that traders wanted to hear a hike today and ONE more in 2019. Traders were buoyed throughout the day as the market climbed higher but then crashed and burned after Powell's speech.

The VIX closed at 25.58 but had been as low as 22.50. Cash was returning to the NASDAQ and NYSE early, but the NYSE started bleeding at around noon with a real cash drawdown after Powell's comments.

"You're a nasty, wasty skunk." From "How the Grinch Stole Christmas."

The S&P opened at 2547 (+1) and reached a high of 2585 (-39) and then skidded to a low of 2489 (-57) before closing at 2507, down 39. Today's low was another 52-week low.

The Dow opened at 23693 (+17) and hit a high of 24057 (+381) before reversing course to hit a new 52 week low of 23163 (-513) before closing at 23324, down 352.

The Nas opened at 6778 (-6) and reached its high of 6869 (+85) and then fell to a low of 6586 (-198) before closing at 6637, down 147. The Nas also hit a new 52 week low.

12/20/18

Today was simply a repeat of previous sessions. The session starts with negative opens followed by a high that was better than the previous close only to end the day with another big loss across the boards.

The VIX did move higher to close at 28.38. The NYSE and NASDAQ continued bleeding through most of

The day as well. "I wouldn't touch you with a thirty-nine-and-a-half foot pole." From "How the Grinch Stole Christmas".

The S&P opened at 2497 (-10) and hit a high of 2510 (+3) and a low of 2441 (-66) before closing at 2467, down 40.

The Dow opened at 23224 (-100) and reached a low of 22644 (-580) before closing at 22860, down 464.

The Nas opened at 6608 (-29) and did hit a high of 6666 (+29) before changing course to hit a low of 6448 (-189) before closing at 6528, down 109.

12/21/18

It was another down day today without any guidance that can be deemed positive for the rest of the year. The VIX closed at 30.11 and double any trader's comfort level and my T/A and P&F sums closed at .128, the lowest level since February 5. Cash continued to bleed from the NYSE and NASDAQ but on a much flatter slope than we have been seeing. "Mr. Gri-inch! Your soul is an appalling dump-heap…". From "How the Grinch Stole Christmas".

The S&P opened at 2465 (-2) and managed a high of 2504 (+37) before dropping to a low of 2409 (-58) and then closing at 2417, down 51.

The Dow opened at 22872 (+12) and hit a high 23255 (+395) and then began a steady slide to a low of 22396 (-464) before closing at 22445, down 414.

The Nas opened at 6573 (+45) and reached a high of 6587 (+59) and proceeded downhill to a low of 6305 (-223) and closed at 6333, down 195.

The S&P began the year at 2674. After today's close it is down 257 points or 9.6%. The Dow started the year at 24719 and is now down 2274 points or 9.2%. The Nas began at 6903 and ended the week down 570 points for the year or 8.3%.

The S&P reached a high of 2941 this year. With Friday's close it is 524 points from its high or 17.8%. The 2018 high for the Dow was 26952. With today's close it is 4507 below its high or 16.7%. The Nas reached a high of 8133 this year and with today's close it is 1800 points below its high or 22.1%.

There are four full trading days left in 2018 and a partial day. I wouldn't be expecting any miracles in such a short trading period which is what it would take to even get to the 2018 opening bell's numbers!

12/24/18

Traders celebrated Christmas Eve at the intersection of Crash and Burnmore instead of the usual Wall and Broad. Although it was a shortened day (close 1 PM), it was enough time for another horrendous day for longs. "You have termites in your smile." From "How the Grinch Stole Christmas".

The VIX reached a high of 36.10 and closed just a shade off at 36.07. My T/A and P&F remained at .12 and cash bled all day but especially heavily in the last ½ hour of the shortened trading day. The major indices are all oversold so a relief rally (dead-cat bounce) is very likely starting some time on Wednesday. Perhaps it will last until Friday or Monday, but I wouldn't bet the farm on that happening.

The S&P opened at 2401 (-16) and reached a closing low of 2351, down 66. It is now down 590 points from its high or 20.1% and in bear territory.

The Dow opened at 22317 (-128) and hit its closing low of 21792, down 653. It is now down 5160 points from its high or 19.1%.

The Nas opened at 6278 (-55) and did manage a high of 6355 (+22) before joining its sister indices to also close lower at 6193, down 140 points. It is now down 1940 points from its high or 23.9%.

The Russell also lost ground closing at its low for the day of 1267, down 25. This index is down 475 points from its high of 1742 or 27.3%.

The Dow is standalone at a correction versus bear territory, but only by 9/10ths of a percent. Will it hold?

12/26/18

Today is the feast of St. Stephen, my namesake. Hopefully, today's market action wasn't a head fake but indeed a relief rally with at least one more day before it ends.

The indices all enjoyed a huge recovery and set records for single day point gains. The S&P was up 117 points (4.96%), and the Dow was up 1086 points (4.98%). The Nas was up 361 points (5.84%) while the Russell finished up 63 points or 4.96%. The Nas and S&P are back in correction territory. This is temporary, so traders will try to make the best of it. A 10% rally over a two day period would be as rare as a Loch

Ness Monster siting but not impossible. Should this happen it might be a good time to close long equity positions.

The S&P opened at 2363 (+12) and hit a low early of 2347 (-4) and then rose steadily through the rest of the session to a closing high of 2468, up 117.

The Dow opened at 21858 (+66) and hit a low of 21713 (-79) before changing direction to hit a high of 22879 (+1087) and closed a fraction off that mark at 22878, up 1086.

And the best performance award goes to the Nas! It opened at 6258 (+65) and cruised to a high of 6556 (+363) before closing a fraction off its high at 6554, up 361 (5.84%).

This a relief rally not a Santa Clause rally and I will be watching tomorrow's action for the least sign of a "okay times-up" rally.

12/27/18

As soon as the markets closed yesterday the futures went south. The indices opened lower this morning, but after yesterday's sharp rise across the board it wasn't a surprise. But the indices all lost ground on an accelerating basis through most of the day closing up in the last half-hour of the session. At one point the indices had given up 60% or more of yesterday's gains. It was another nail-biter kind of day.

The VIX closed at 29.69. It has been above 30 since the 20th. Cas continued bleeding from the NYSE and NASDAQ with some recovery in the final minutes of trading. My T/A and P&F sums are still closing in the hinterlands.

The S&P opened at 2442 (-26) and reached a low of 2398 (-70) before rebounding to close at its high of 2489, up 21.

The Dow opened at 22629 (-249) ang hit a low of 22267 (-611) before changing course to close at its high of 23139, up 260.

The Nas opened at 6457 (-97) and saw a low of 6337 (-217) before climbing to a high of 6583 (+29). It closed at 6579, up 25.

12/28/18

Today was about as choppy as it gets. It was the last full trading day of the year, the week, month and quarter. Many market makers and traders remained away from their desks while fund managers were trying to put "lipstick on their pig" in order to prepare their clients for the inevitable bad news that will be their quarterly reports.

The VIX dropped some to 28.34, down 1.62. It is basically a meaningless drop and likely will spend more time in the thirties in the immediate future. My T/A and P&F sums improved but remain below 1. I won't get excited about trading until it has been over 1 for at least seven to ten days. The staff at StockCharts.com is in concurrence that there is further downside risk.

The S&P opened at 2499 (+10) and ranged from a low of 2473 (-16) to a high of 2520 (+31) before closing at 2486, down 3.

The Dow opened at 23214 (+75) and hit a low of 22981 (-158) and a high of 23382 (+243) but moved lower to close at 23062, down 76.

The Nas opened at 6617 (+38) and reached a low of 6529 (-50) before recovering to close at 6585, up 5. The Nas and Russell were the only major indices to close up. The Russell gained 6 to close at 1338.

12/31/18

I doubt that many traders are disappointed to see this quarter and year end. Perhaps some short traders did well but I doubt many longs did. Being a member of Stockcharts and reading the blogs daily has kept me out of trouble although I still lost on trades this quarter.

The VIX closed at 25.42, down 2.92 from yesterday but still too high for comfort. Cash continued bleeding from the NYSE and NASDAQ as well. This direction has to obviously change before this bear market can end. My T/A and P&F sums remained below 1 as should be expected.

The S&P opened at 2499 (+13) and hit a morning low of 2483 (-3) and a high of 2509 (+23) before closing at 2507, op 21.

The Dow opened at 23154 (+92) and hit a high of 23333 (+271) before closing at 23327, up 265.

The Nas opened at 6650 (+65) and reached a morning low of 6570 (-15) and an afternoon high of 6660 (+75) before closing at 6635, up 51.

The S&P began the year at 2674. With today's close it lost 167 points or -6.2% for the year. The high for the year was 2941. With today's close it was down 434 points from its high or -14.8%.

The Dow started the year at 24719. With today's close it is down 1392 points or -5.6%. The Dow's high for the year was 26952. With today's close it ended 3625 points below its high or -13.4%.

The Nas opened the year at 6903. With today's close it was down 268 points for the year or -3.9%. The high for the year was 8133. With today's close it is 1498 points off that high or -18.4%

These three indices are in correction as the year comes to a close.

I committed to keeping a daily journal of the index data points for the S&P, Dow and NASDAQ (Nas) at the end of last year. It helped me to pay more attention to the markets, particularly after closing my ICMA accounts into our Fidelity IRA. As the new year unfolds, I am long in BOIL, CLVS and GDX and don't intend to change these positions because of the high VIX and my belief that we are in a bear market.

Glossary

COB	Close of Business (Day)
Dow	Dow Jones Industrial Average
EMA	Exponential Moving Average
FED	Federal Reserve Board
ICMA-RC	International City Management Association Retirement Corporation
Nas	My abbreviation for the NASDAQ Composite
NASDAQ	Initially an acronym for National Association of Securities Dealers Automated Quotations
NG	Natural Gas
NYSE	New York Stock Exchange
PLUS Fund	A stable value/cash management fund for 401 & 457 plans
P&F	Point and Figure Patterns
PMO	Decision Point Price Momentum Oscillator
PPO	Percentage Price Oscillator
REIT	Real Estate Investment Trust
RSI	Relative Strength Index
Russell	Refers to the Russell 2000 Index
S&P	Standard and Poor's 500 Index
SMA	Simple Moving Average
T/A	Technical Analysis Indicators
VIX	CBOE Volatility Index
WTIC	West Texas Intermediate Crude

Made in United States
North Haven, CT
04 November 2026

21772139R00062